# JO VERSO'S COMPLETE CROSS STITCH COURSE

✕ ✕ ✕ ✕ ✕

# JO VERSO'S
## COMPLETE
## CROSS STITCH
## COURSE

David & Charles

# MATERIALS & EQUIPMENT

*Before you can get started you will
need to assemble some basic supplies.
Photographed on the following pages are many of the
most readily available materials, but you will
probably never use the full range on offer. Each skill
in the book will list the specific materials required
to work the project.*

# FABRICS

On entering a good needlecraft shop you will find a bewildering array of embroidery fabrics. Disregard the canvas section: canvas is used for needlepoint and canvas work. Look for the Aida and evenweave fabrics on which cross stitch is worked.

Cross stitch fabrics are classified either by a thread count number, ie, how many threads or blocks there are to 1in (2.5cm), or by an HPI (holes per inch) number, ie, how many holes there are to 1in (2.5cm). These two terms are the same and will tell you how many cross stitches to 1in (2.5cm) you will work on the fabric. The lower the count, the coarser the fabric and the larger the cross stitch will be. Conversely, the higher the count, the finer the fabric and the smaller the cross stitch will be.

Each design in this book tells you which fabric to work on and how much is needed, but if a pattern in another publication gives you no guidance and you are bewildered by the choice of fabrics, choose a fabric which suits your pocket, feels good to handle and which has a thread count that is not too fine for your eyesight.

## Aida Fabric
Aida, produced by Permin and Zweigart, is a widely available cotton fabric in which threads are packed together during the weaving process to form blocks.

These blocks form easy-to-see squares and each cross stitch is worked over one block. The coarsest is 6 count Binca which is cut into squares mainly for children. Other Aida fabrics come in various colours and counts – 8, 11, 14, 16 and 18 HPI or blocks to 1in (2.5cm) being most common.

Some Aidas are shot with Lurex to add sparkle to special occasions and some, like Rustico, are flecked to give a rustic appearance. Easy-count Aida has a contrasting thread woven into it at regular intervals to assist counting; when work is complete this thread is easily removed without any disturbance to the stitching.

Damask fabrics, for table cloths and cushions, are available with areas of Aida woven into them at regular intervals. Aida bands or ribbons come in a variety of widths and with plain or decorative edges; when stitched these have many uses and can decorate a multitude of household items.

Aida can be bought by the metre or, often, as small offcuts. It is an ideal fabric for beginners, having the advantages of being readily available and the holes being easy to see and count.

*Opposite The count of the fabric determines the size of the design, as these Aida samples show.*

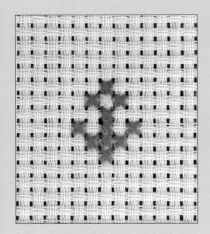

*6 count Binca, 100% cotton*

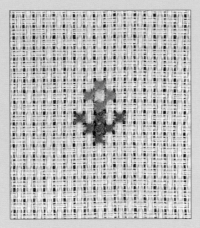

*8 count Aida, 100% cotton*

*11 count Aida, 100% cotton*

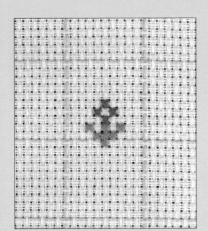

*11 count Easy-Count Aida,
98% cotton, 2% polyester*

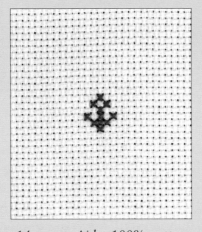

*14 count Aida, 100% cotton*

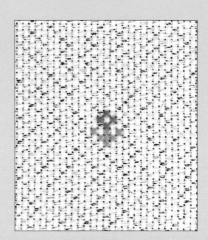

*14 count Lurex Aida,
93% cotton, 7% Lurex*

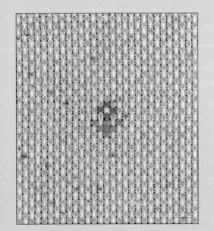

*14 count Rustico Aida, 51%
cotton, 34% viscose, 15% linen*

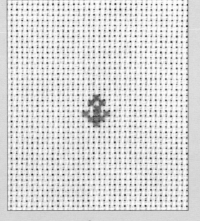

*16 count Aida, 100% cotton*

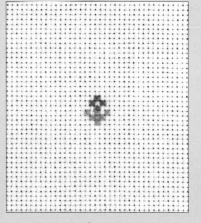

*18 count Aida, 100% cotton*

*A selection of Aida and evenweave bands.*

## Evenweave Fabric

Evenweave fabric is woven with single threads and is called evenweave because there are the same number of weft (horizontal) threads as there are warp (vertical) threads to 1in (2.5cm). If the fabric is not evenweave then the design will be distorted as you stitch it and is therefore unsuitable. When using an evenweave fabric the cross stitch is worked over two threads, so an evenweave with 20 threads to 1in (2.5cm) will produce 10 cross stitches to 1in (2.5cm). There are many thread counts available in evenweave and a large choice of colours.

Common evenweaves are Zweigart Linda (cotton) and Jobelan (cotton/viscose mix), but the Rolls Royce of evenweave fabrics is evenweave linen with its excellent qualities of durability and handling. Permin produce a large range of evenweave linens and Zweigart produce the popular Dublin, Belfast and Edinburgh linens.

As evenweave linen is woven from natural fibres, some of the threads are coarser than others, but by working the cross stitch over two threads any discrepancies are evened out.

Zweigart Oslo is also available. This is a Hardanger fabric which has the advantage for beginners of a low thread count but the appearance of a fine fabric. This is because Hardanger fabrics are double rather than single weave, so the cross stitch is worked over two pairs of threads.

## Other Materials

The projects in this book will give you the chance to work with various materials as follows. ***Plastic canvas*** which can be cut and assembled into three-dimensional objects. ***Perforated paper,*** for delicate work, can be folded and cut without the edges fraying. ***Aida Plus*** is like perforated paper but less fragile. ***Waste canvas*** can be applied to almost any fabric to make it suitable for cross stitching. ***Silk gauze*** allows for very fine work in miniature.

Opposite *Various evenweave fabric counts.*

20 count Zweigart Bellana,
52% cotton, 48% viscose

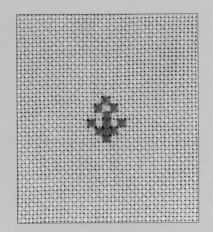

22 count Zweigart Oslo
Hardanger, 100% cotton

25 count Zweigart Dublin
linen, 100% linen

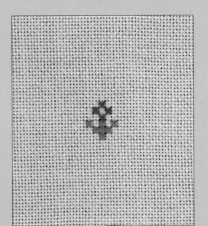

27 count Zweigart Linda,
100% cotton

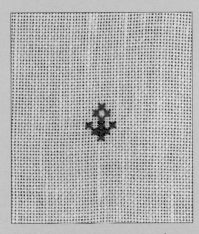

28 count Zweigart Quaker
Cloth, 55% linen, 45% cotton

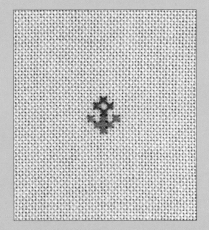

28 count Jobelan, 51%
cotton, 49% viscose

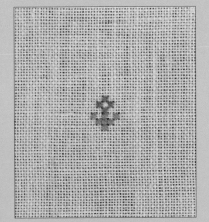

32 count Zweigart Belfast
linen, 100% linen

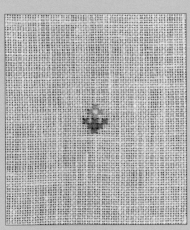

36 count Zweigart Edinburgh
linen, 100% linen

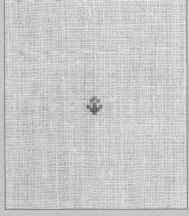

55 count Zweigart Kingston
linen, 100% linen

## Calculating How Much Fabric to Buy

You will need a piece of fabric large enough to accommodate your stitched design, with enough spare fabric all round the edges to allow at least 2in (5cm) for turnings to be made when the embroidery is framed or made up.

   To calculate the fabric size, first count the number of squares horizontally and vertically on your design. Then divide the number of squares by the number of cross stitches produced per inch (2.5cm) of your chosen fabric.

*For example*:
*Your design has 110 squares by 99.*
*Your chosen fabric is 11 count Aida, so you will get 11 cross stitches to 1in (2.5cm).*
*110 divided by 11 = 10.*
*99 divided by 11 = 9.*

*Your finished embroidery will measure 10 x 9in (25.5 x 23cm) and to this you need to add a turning allowance of 2in (5cm) all round. Therefore the piece of fabric you need to cut should measure 14 x 13in (35.5 x 33cm).*

   Remember to divide the thread count of an evenweave fabric by 2 to arrive at the number of cross stitches per 1in (2.5cm): for example, a 28 count evenweave will produce 14 cross stitches per 1in (2.5cm).

To check whether your embroidery will fit a chosen mount, for example when working a greetings card, calculate the finished size of the embroidery as described above. If too large to fit the mount, work on a finer fabric with a higher count. If too small, work on a coarser fabric with a lower count.

# THREADS

There is a large range of threads available for cross stitching today and the thoughtful choice of colour and type of thread can enhance a piece of work greatly.

## Stranded Cotton

This is the most commonly used thread for working counted cross stitch onto the background fabric. DMC, Anchor and Madeira all produce excellent stranded cottons in every colour imaginable. Stranded cottons are bought by the skein, each skein containing 8 metres of mercerised six-stranded cotton. It is easiest to work with an 18in (45cm) length cut from the skein. Single strands can then be removed to form groups of two, three or more strands as required, to achieve many different effects.

## Flower Threads

Flower threads, produced by DMC and the Danish Handcraft Guild, are made from 100 per cent cotton and are non-divisible. Whereas stranded cottons have a lustrous finish, flower thread has a matt finish and is suitable when a softer effect might be desired.

## Metallic Thread

Metallic thread can be used to add glitter and interest to the embroidery. DMC produce a range of soft metallic threads suitable for cross stitch embroidery. Kreinik Metallics Balger blending filament is ideal for projects which require a lot of sparkle.

Many threads are set out to tempt you in a needlework shop. Crewel wools are not used for traditional cross stitch embroidery, but rules were made to be broken and interesting experiments can be made when you are feeling more adventurous. Different threads, such as Marlitt and Coton Perlé will produce different effects, so do not reject thread until you have tried working a few stitches with it.

## How Many Strands of Thread?

Usually, the pattern you are working will tell you how many strands of thread you should be working with – that is, sufficient to give good coverage of the fabric but not so many that they will distort the holes. As a general rule, for 10–13 cross stitches to 1in (2.5cm) use three strands of stranded cotton. For 14–18 cross stitches to 1in (2.5cm) use two strands of stranded cotton. Back stitch and French knots are generally worked with one strand only. If in doubt try a few sample stitches in the corner of your fabric to check coverage.

# CROSS STITCHER'S TOOLS

The following equipment is essential for counted cross stitch. Buy the best quality you can afford, treat your investment with care and it should last for many years.

## Tapestry Needles

Use a blunt tapestry needle and choose one that slips easily through the holes in your fabric without piercing or splitting the threads. Finer needles have a higher number on the packet (26, 24); thicker needles have lower numbers (22, 18).

To embellish cross stitch with beads, attach these using a beading needle. These are also available in different sizes but are finer, with a sharp point.

## Embroidery Scissors

You will need sharp, fine-pointed scissors to cut lengths of stranded cotton from the skein and to trim off finished threads on the back of the work. To preserve their sharpness never cut fabric or paper with them – scissors which are not sharp enough will chew the thread and make a mess. Wear your scissors on a ribbon around your neck to keep them always to hand.

## Embroidery Frames

For pieces of work which are too large to fit into embroidery hoops, these consist of two wooden stretchers at the side and two wooden rollers at the top and bottom, held in place with wing-nuts or pegs. The rollers each have a piece of webbing fixed to them onto which the fabric is stitched.

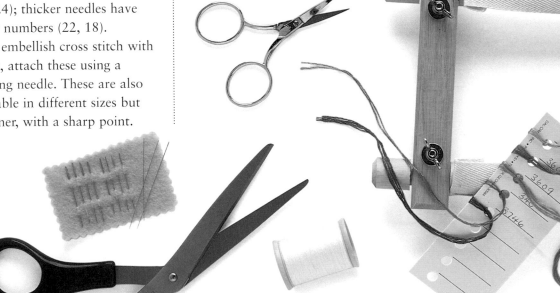

## Dressmaking Scissors

You will need these to cut your fabric to size before sewing.

## Sewing Thead

This is used to oversew the edges of your fabric to prevent fraying. It is also used to tack the central lines on the fabric. Do not be tempted to use dark coloured sewing thread for tacking as it can leave slight traces of fibres to discolour your fabric.

## Thread Organiser

Keep spare strands of embroidery thread on a thread organiser to keep them in order. You can make your own by punching holes down the side of one of those pieces of card from inside a packet of tights.

## Embroidery and Flexi-Hoops

Embroidery and flexi-hoops are used to hold the fabric taut whilst stitching and are necessary to produce even stitching. Use a hoop only if the area to be stitched fits easily inside it. If the hoop has to be moved over existing embroidery the stitches risk being flattened and distorted by the pressure of the hoop.

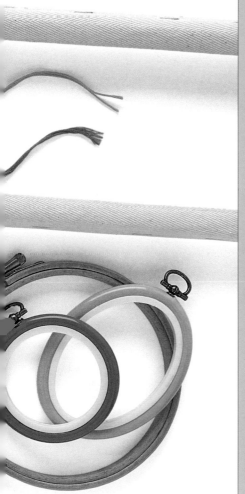

## Useful But Not Crucial Equipment

The following equipment can be acquired as and when you wish, or put your chosen items on your Christmas list.

• *Unpicking scissors* have a neat little hook in the bottom blade which assists the removal of offending threads.

• *Table or floor-standing frames* allow you to have one hand at the front of the work and one at the back, speeding work up considerably.

• *Gold-plated needles* are sheer self indulgence for some but a boon for those whose body chemistry removes the plating from an ordinary tapestry needle.

• *Stitching gloves* prevent the hands getting tired as you stitch.

• *A Stitch catcher* is a natty little gadget which allows you to use even the last tiny piece of thread before it runs out.

• *Needle threaders* are useful if your eyesight isn't great and there is nobody around to thread the needle for you.

• *A Work stand* allows you to clamp a hoop or frame to it, leaving both hands free to work.

• *Chart holders* are magnetic boards used in conjunction with magnetic chart markers to help you keep your place on a chart.

• *Daylight bulbs* can be used in most lamps to give a good light for stitching at night or on dull days.

• *Magnifiers* can keep us stitching happily when eyesight is failing. They range from a pair of strong spectacles to floor-standing magnifiers with built-in lights. Line magnifiers can be placed over charts to make them easier to read. Magnifiers are available which hang around your neck, or which clip onto your existing spectacles. For cross stitch embroidery to be enjoyable you have to be able to see what you are doing.

• *Shade cards* available from thread manufacturers are invaluable if you progress to choosing your own shades of thread for projects. Colours are grouped into 'families' of different depths of each shade, so, if you want, for example, a light, medium and dark blue which tone well, choose them from a suitable blue family. You can see at a glance all available shades which also assists choice.

# GETTING STARTED

*Once you have assembled the materials for your
project you will be eager to start stitching at once.
But do take time to set the work up correctly as careful
preparation at this stage can make all the difference
to the quality of your finished masterpiece.*

✕ ✕ ✕ ✕

## PREPARING THE FABRIC

1 Cut the fabric to the size stated in the You Will
Need section of the project instructions. When
working designs from other books or magazines
and no size is stated, you must ensure that you have
allowed enough fabric for the design (pg12), plus
2in (5cm) all round to allow for mounting. When
cutting the fabric use sharp dressmaking scissors: do
not be tempted to use your embroidery scissors –
these should only be used to cut embroidery thread.
If possible, make a note of where the selvedge edges
are on the fabric piece and aim to have these on the
left and right of the design as it is stitched as this
will make the stretching of the finished piece a
little easier.

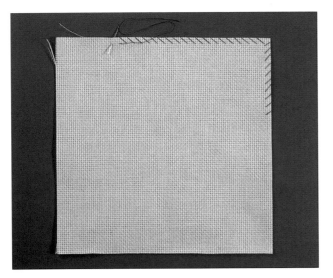

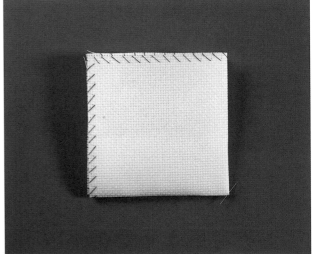

2 Oversew the edges of the fabric to prevent
fraying: this can be done by hand or on a
sewing machine using a zigzag stitch. Frayed
threads at the edge of the work can get tangled up
with embroidery thread on the back and are a
nuisance. Before you start to stitch, iron the fabric
to remove any stubborn creases.

3 Find the centre of the fabric as this is where the
first stitch will be worked. Stitching the central
stitch of a design in the centre of the fabric ensures
that there will be an even amount of spare fabric all
round the design which is important at the
mounting stage. Fold the fabric into four and mark
the central point temporarily with a pin.

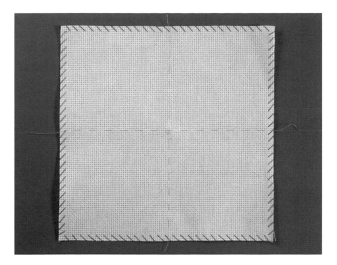

4 Using light-coloured tacking thread mark the vertical and horizontal lines which meet in the centre of the fabric. Remove the pin. Once the cross stitching is complete, the tacking threads will be removed.

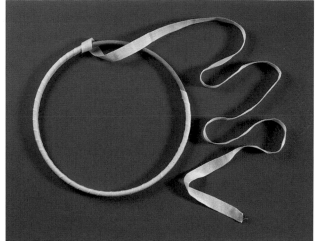

## USING AN EMBROIDERY HOOP
### (STEPS 5 – 7)

5 Mount the fabric in a hoop large enough to contain the whole design: moving a hoop around over existing stitches will crush and distort them. First, bind the inner hoop with a white bias cotton tape to protect the fabric and prevent slipping.

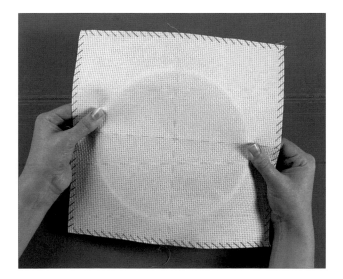

6 Lay the fabric over the inner hoop ring, positioning it so that the centre of the fabric lies in the centre of the hoop.

7 Place the outer ring of the hoop over the inner ring, with the tension screw at the top out of the way. Press the outer hoop down over the inner and tighten the tension screw, adjusting the fabric so that it is taut as a drum. Check that the horizontal and vertical threads have not been distorted in the process. Reposition the fabric if they have.

## Using a Flexi-hoop

8 Flexi-hoops are circular or oval, plastic hoops which consist of a rigid inner hoop and a flexible outer hoop. The outer hoop is eased onto the inner hoop to hold work tautly in place. Flexi-hoops come in a variety of sizes, colours and finishes. Because they are available in very small sizes, they are often used instead of wooden embroidery hoops for working very small projects like the Chatelaine pincushion (pg48). When stitching is finished, the flexi-hoop can be used as a decorative frame for the completed work (see Ringing the Changes, pg110).

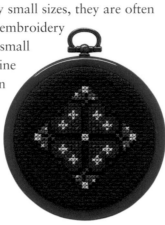

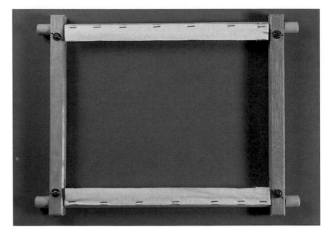

## Using an Embroidery Frame
### (steps 9 – 11)

9 If the design you are working is too large to fit a hoop, use an embroidery frame. First, hem your fabric to strengthen the edges so that it will not pull apart when it is laced to the frame.

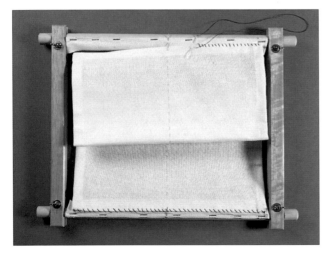

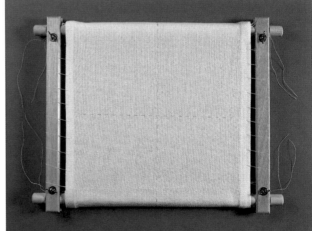

10 Sew the top of the fabric to the top piece of the frame's webbing, and do the same at the bottom, matching the centre of the fabric to the centre of the webbing. Do not be tempted to use drawing pins or staples to attach the fabric – threads may be pulled which will ruin the fabric.

11 Lace the sides of the fabric to the frame stretchers with strong thread and, when both sides are laced, tighten the threads and the wing-nuts so that the fabric is stretched taut. Tie the ends of the threads firmly to the stretchers. When working a long design it may be necessary to roll completed stitching onto one of the rollers to expose more fabric for work. In this case a sheet of white tissue paper rolled into the back of the work will prevent crushing the stitches.

## USING WASTE FABRIC (STEPS 12 – 13)

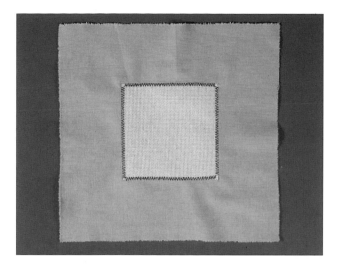

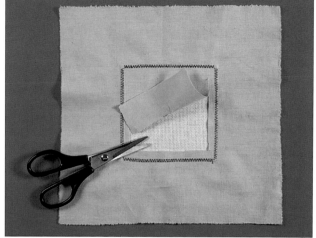

12 When working very tiny designs it can be wasteful to cut a piece of embroidery fabric large enough to fit a hoop. If this is the case, cut a piece of waste fabric large enough to fit the hoop. Cut a piece of embroidery fabric to the required size and stitch this firmly to the centre of the waste fabric.

13 Cut away the waste fabric from behind the embroidery fabric. Turn the fabric to the right side and mount into a hoop as usual. When the embroidery is complete the rest of the waste fabric is trimmed away and discarded.

## THREADING THE NEEDLE (STEPS 14 – 15)

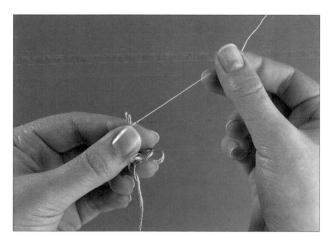

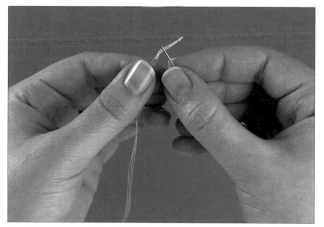

14 To thread the needle to begin stitching select the colour indicated by the chart for the centre of the design. Gently pull an 18in (45cm) length from your skein of stranded cotton and cut it off. Remove the required number of strands from the cut length of stranded cotton one at a time.

15 Lay the removed threads side by side and stroke them to remove any twists. The less twists you have on the thread, the better the stitches will cover the fabric. Thread the needle and you are ready to work your first cross stitch.

# READING A CHART

Cross stitch designs are available where the pattern is printed directly onto the fabric and the cross stitches are worked to cover the printing. The resulting cross stitches tend to be uneven and rather hit-and-miss, so results can be disappointing. Far more popular now are designs for counted cross stitch which is the subject of this book. Counted cross stitch is worked from charts, and each square on the chart, whether stitched or unstitched, represents one block of Aida or two threads of evenweave fabric. It is therefore important to be able to understand a chart and be able to translate it into stitching.

All the charts in this book are printed in colour so that you can see at a glance which colour to use for each stitch. To help further, each coloured square carries a symbol to clarify the exact colour required. If two different shades of one colour are used the symbols help to distinguish between them. If you wish to make your work easier to carry with you, the symbols make it possible to take a black and white photocopy of a colour chart which can then be coloured in using crayons if you find this helpful. All the charts have a colour key which tells

you which colour thread corresponds to the colours marked on the chart.

It is important to find the central stitch in the chart as this is the first stitch worked in the centre of the fabric. Many charts will have arrows indicating the central point, others will mark the central point with an asterisk or other mark, such as the five-pointed star on my charts. If a chart is not marked in this way, find the centre by counting the squares in each direction and dividing them by two. You can then mark the centre for yourself.

You may have come across designs that have an unworked square or squares in the centre. In this case, count the empty squares on the chart outwards from the centre to the first area of stitching indicated. On the fabric, count the same number of blank blocks/pairs of threads outwards from the centre to find the corresponding position to start stitching.

Opposite *This chart shows the various symbols used to indicate specific stitches.*
Below *This chart shows the use of a colour key for threads used.*

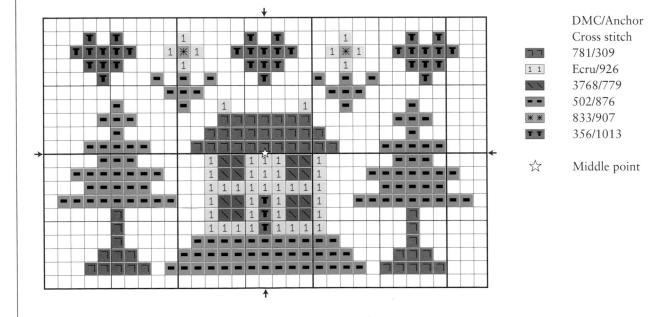

| | DMC/Anchor |
|---|---|
| | Cross stitch |
| ⊓⊓ | 781/309 |
| 1 1 | Ecru/926 |
| ＼＼ | 3768/779 |
| ▬▬ | 502/876 |
| ✳✳ | 833/907 |
| T T | 356/1013 |
| ☆ | Middle point |

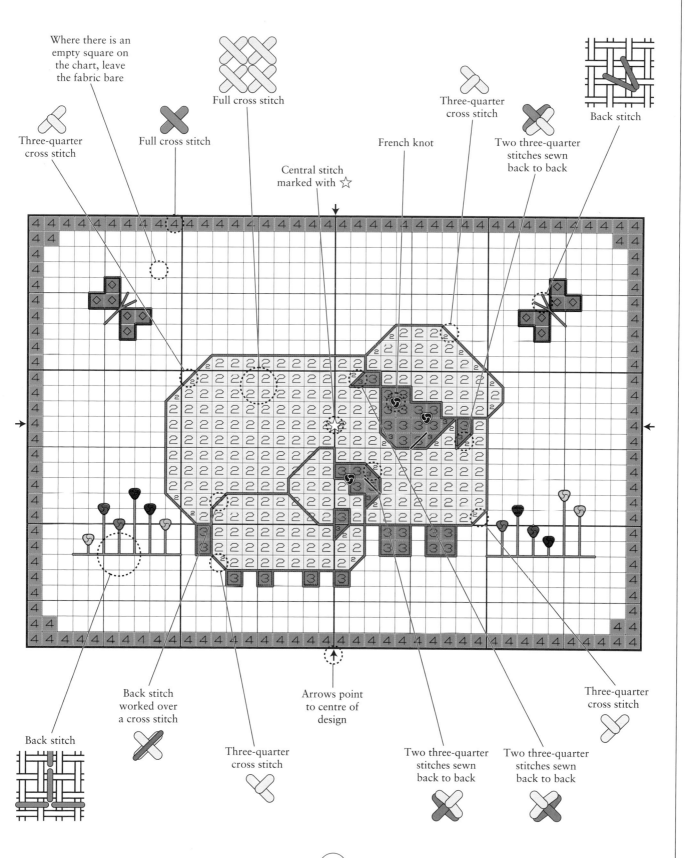

Where there is an empty square on the chart, leave the fabric bare

Full cross stitch

Three-quarter cross stitch

Back stitch

Three-quarter cross stitch

Full cross stitch

Central stitch marked with ☆

French knot

Two three-quarter stitches sewn back to back

Back stitch worked over a cross stitch

Arrows point to centre of design

Three-quarter cross stitch

Back stitch

Three-quarter cross stitch

Two three-quarter stitches sewn back to back

Two three-quarter stitches sewn back to back

Three-quarter cross stitch

# FULL CROSS STITCH

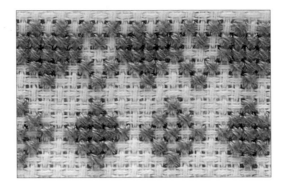

*The stitch which forms the basis of counted cross stitch, and which you will use most frequently, is the full cross stitch. Crosses are formed in two stages to produce a stitch which is square in shape and which corresponds to the squares on the graph paper of your charted pattern.*

## NEEDLE CASE

*Finished Size: (folded) 4½ x 3¼in (11.5 x 8cm)*

Your first pattern has been designed so that the first row of cross stitches you work is a simple straight line. Each line thereafter requires a little more skill but builds on what you have just learned. The stitching is in a single colour to ensure minimum outlay on materials and to allow you to concentrate on the stitches themselves. So that none of your effort is wasted, your first steps in cross stitch can be made into a useful and decorative needle case in which to keep your cross stitch needles. By changing the colour of the background fabric and thread, a totally different effect can be achieved from the same design as you can see by comparing the finished needle case pictured opposite with that on pg29.

### You Will Need
- *7in (18cm) embroidery hoop*
- *11 x 11in (28 x 28cm) 11 count Aida fabric, in White or Sky*
- *5½ x 4¼in (14 x 11cm) 11 count Aida fabric, in White or Sky*
- *Stranded cotton in Blue (see colour key) or White*
- *Tapestry needle, size 24*
- *10 x 4¼in (25.5 x 11cm) cotton backing fabric*
- *White sewing thread*
- *30in (76cm) cotton lace or braid for trimming*
- *Short length of 3mm ribbon to make into a bow*
- *8½ x 3in (21.5 x 7.5cm) white felt*

1 Prepare the larger piece of Aida fabric for work (pg16). Mount the fabric into the hoop (pg17), then thread the needle (pg19). Starting at the centre of the chart, match it to the centre of your fabric which has already been marked with tacking thread.

### THE KNOTLESS START
### (STEPS 2 – 6)

*Use this method of starting when working with uneven numbers of strands of thread in the needle. It forms a flat, neat start without a bulging knot on the back of the work which can form an unsightly lump.*

2 Though it sounds like a contradiction, tie a knot in the end of your three-stranded length of cotton and insert the needle on the right side of the fabric approximately 1½in (3.5cm) to the right of the centre. Bring the needle up at the starting position of Row 1 marked ☆ on the chart.

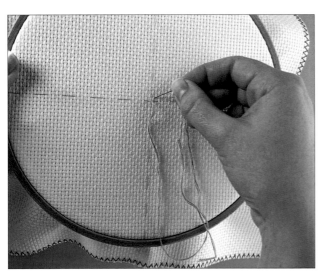

3 Insert the needle in the top right-hand hole of the block thus forming half a cross stitch.

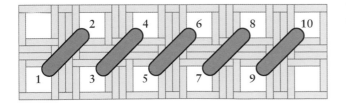

4 Bring the needle out at the bottom left-hand hole of the next block and insert it in the top right-hand hole of that block. Continue to form half crosses going from left to right (see diagram, left).

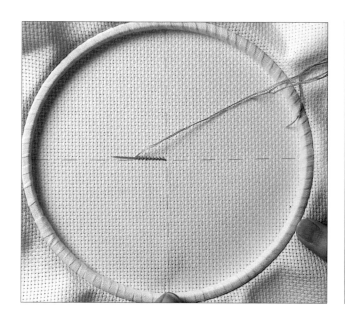

**5** As you continue this way, secure the laid thread on the back of the work as you go.

**6** When it is secure, cut off the knot on the front of the work and trim the tail on the back.

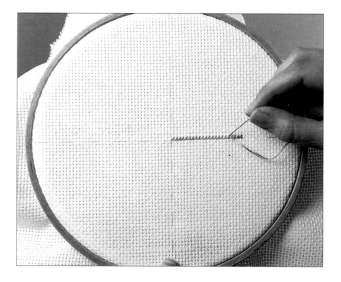

**7** Working from right to left, cross each stitch using the same holes as before, but stitching

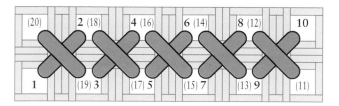

### Perfectionist's Corner

*Always work the first half of all full cross stitches in the same direction. This ensures that all top stitches will lie in the same direction, giving an even appearance and uniform sheen to the work. It does not matter whether your bottom stitch goes from bottom left to top right, or from bottom right to top left, so long as you are consistent. Beware of turning work in your hand to work the side of a border, for instance – a large cross stitch worked in the corner of your fabric will serve as an instant reference.*

from bottom right to top left of each block. All cross stitches 'hold hands' and share holes with their neighbours (see diagram, left). Finish Row 1 by stitching the remaining cross stitches which lie to the left of the starting position, ensuring all bottom stitches lie in the same direction.

## THE KNOTLESS FINISH (STEPS 8 – 9)
*This method finishes a thread neatly, again avoiding unsightly knots and lumps.*

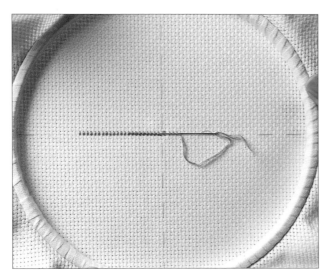

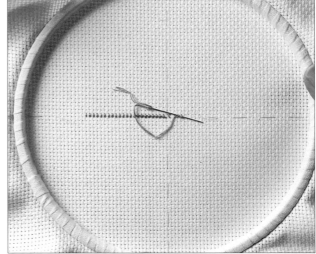

**8** On the back of the work thread the needle through the back of the last three stitches worked.

**9** Return, jumping over one stitch and threading the needle through the back of two stitches. Trim the thread neatly, close to the stitching, using sharp embroidery scissors.

## JOINING A NEW THREAD (STEPS 10 – 11)

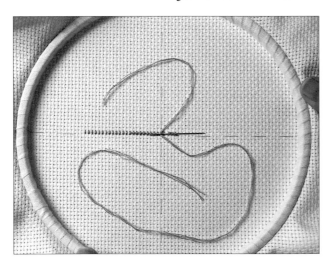

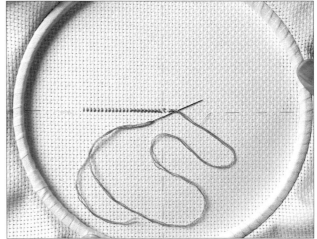

**10** To join a new thread where there arc existing stitches, pass the needle through the back of three stitches on the back of the work as close as possible to where you want to start stitching again.

**11** Take a back stitch into the last stitch to secure the thread and bring the needle to the front of the work ready to continue stitching.

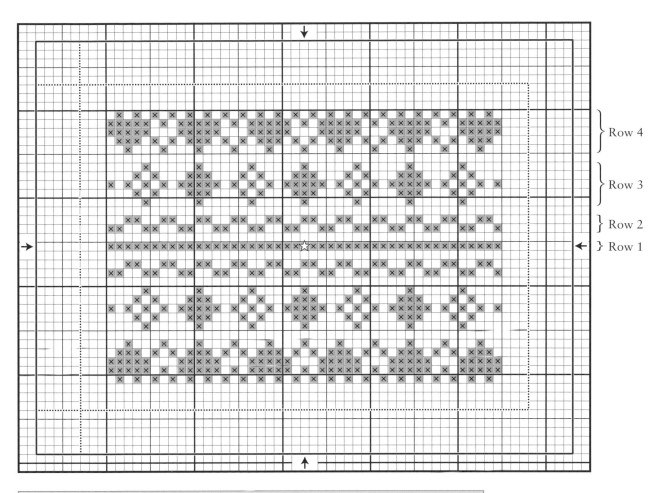

Row 4

Row 3

Row 2

Row 1

## Emergency Unpicking Kit

*Check frequently that your counting is correct; whilst one hesitates to mention the ghastly word 'unpicking', it is something which has to be done by even the most proficient cross stitchers from time to time. To help avoid it, count your stitches carefully as you work, and re-check frequently as work progresses. The few minutes it takes are well spent and could save hours of work later. Never be tempted to use a stitch ripper as this will pull and distort neighbouring stitches.*

*To make the task easier equip yourself with a pair of unpicking scissors. The tiny hook at the end of the bottom blade allows the offending stitch to be lifted for cutting and removal. Tweezers can assist you to remove the threads and Sellotape helps to remove traces of fluff. Unpicking dark thread from light fabric is rarely successful as microscopic fibres remain in the holes and leave a dark shadow for ever more.*

## NEEDLE CASE

### Colour Key

|  | DMC/Anchor |
|---|---|
| ×× | 3755/140 |
| ........ | Seam lines |
| — | Cutting line |
| ☆ | Middle point |

### NOTES

Use three strands of stranded cotton to work all the cross stitches.

**12** Work the required number of cross stitches to the end of the line, as indicated on the chart, counting your stitches and matching them to the squares on the chart on pg27.

**13** *Row 2* Work the stitches in the order suggested in the lower diagram right. The figures in brackets indicate that the needle is to be inserted from the front of the work to the back. Frequently with full cross stitch a situation will arise where, in order to keep the bottom stitches lying in the same direction, a more complicated route has to be worked to ensure that existing stitches are not undone. The stitch between holes 5 and 6 is a good example. If it was worked in the same direction as

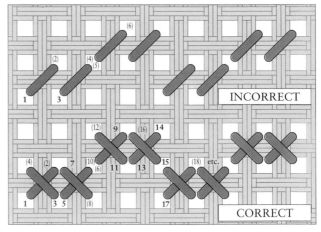

the first two stitches, then the stitch between 3 and 4 would be undone. The working order shown above is therefore recommended.

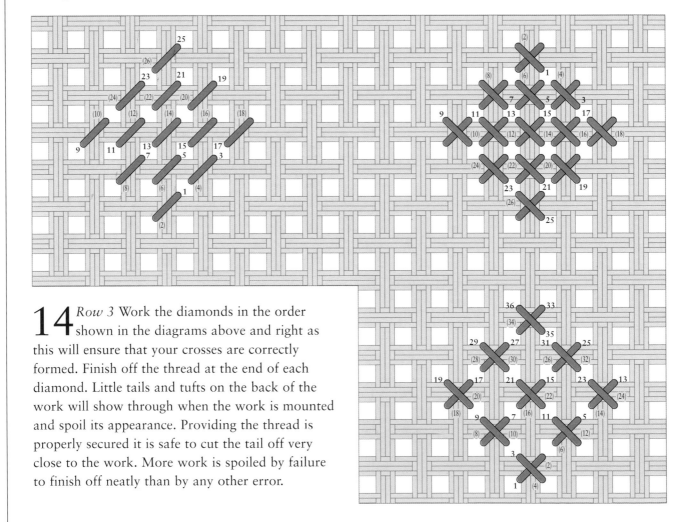

**14** *Row 3* Work the diamonds in the order shown in the diagrams above and right as this will ensure that your crosses are correctly formed. Finish off the thread at the end of each diamond. Little tails and tufts on the back of the work will show through when the work is mounted and spoil its appearance. Providing the thread is properly secured it is safe to cut the tail off very close to the work. More work is spoiled by failure to finish off neatly than by any other error.

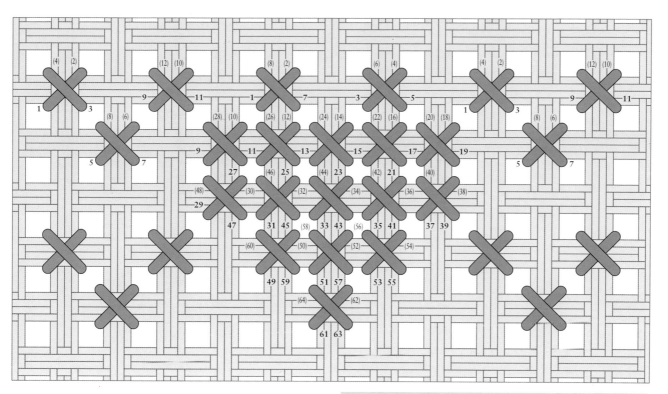

**15** *Row 4* Work the solid hearts first in the order shown in the diagram above. Rejoin the thread to the back of a worked heart (pg26), then work the top three linking cross stitches. Continue working in this way to the end of the row. Follow the same procedure to work the linking stitches at the bottom.

## Perfectionist's Corner

*Plan the route of your stitching very carefully. Always aim to run the thread away from a hole at an angle which forms a neat cross. Diagram A below shows a cross stitch correctly formed, where the thread has been taken from hole 4 in any of the directions shown by the arrows. Diagram B shows a cross stitch with an untidy long 'leg' formed by taking the thread forwards to the next hole. On occasions it may appear that more thread is used on the back of the work, but it is a false economy to sacrifice the appearance of the work for a few inches of thread.*

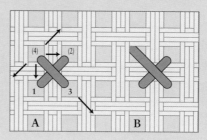

## MAKING UP THE NEEDLE CASE (STEPS 16 – 22)

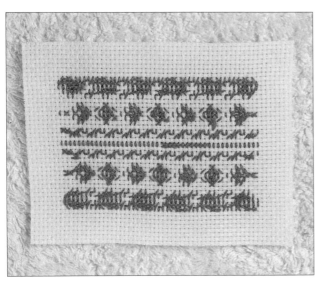

**16** Remove the work from the hoop, then unpick and discard the tacking threads. Trim the embroidered fabric (the front of the needle case) to the size shown on the chart. If necessary, press the finished work.

**17** To do this, lay a thick, fluffy, white terry towel on a flat surface (see boxed text opposite). Place your embroidery face down on the towel and cover it with a clean, white cotton cloth. Iron the work with a moderately hot iron.

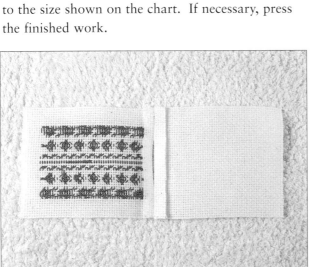

**18** Cut the smaller piece of Aida (the back of the needle case) to the same size as the front. Place the two pieces of fabric right sides together, and using sewing thread seam them together with a back stitch or a machine straight stitch leaving a 2in (5cm) opening at the centre of the seam. Press the seam open.

**19** Place the embroidery and the cotton backing fabric right sides together and using sewing thread stitch around the seam line. Clip the corners and trim the seam allowance to ¼in (6mm) and turn right side out.

### Pressing Embroidery

Sometimes it is necessary to iron finished work. Using a thick, fluffy, white terry towel allows the stitches to sink into the pile so that they are not flattened whilst the back of the work is pressed. Pressing stitches on a hard surface risks ruining them, making them flat and lifeless.

**20** Use neat and tiny slip stitches to close the opening.

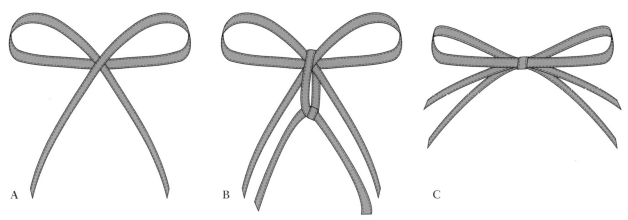

A      B      C

**21** Trim the outer edges of the needle case with lace or braid. Add a small bow of ribbon as the finishing touch. To make the bow, cut a length of ribbon and fold to form two loops as shown in diagram A above. Cut another length of ribbon and knot it around the centre as in diagram B above. Pull the knot tight, tease into shape and trim ends as in diagram C above.

**22** Cut a leaf of felt to hold the needles; for a decorative finish cut the felt with pinking shears. Fold the needle case and the leaf of felt in half and stitch the leaf of felt to the inside of the needle case along the crease.

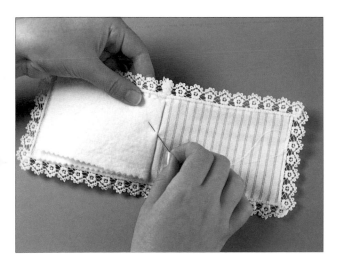

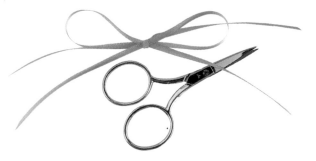

# MULTICOLOURED CROSS STITCH

*There are hundreds of shades of stranded cottons from which to choose and as you progress you will acquire a wide selection of colours. The choice may seem bewildering at first, but whether a pattern requires only a few colours or a multitude, the harmonious use of colour is one of the great joys of cross stitch.*

# BOOKMARK
*Finished Size: 7½ x 2in (19 x 5cm)*

Just five shades of stranded cotton have been used for this project, simplicity being the key. Two shades of pink, two of mauve and a green are combined to make a pretty bookmark, giving you practise at changing colours in cross stitch. As an exercise in colour selection, try working the pattern in different colour combinations; you will soon discover what works and what does not.

When choosing colours for yourself, place the skeins on the fabric which you are going to use, as the background can affect the colours. If one or some of the colours are not harmonious they will stand out and beg to be changed. If you are very unsure of your ability to pick colours, make a note of colour combinations that please you in other people's work, magazines, books and so on, and use these colours in your own projects.

### You Will Need
- 8in (20cm) embroidery hoop
- 12 x 12in (30.5 x 30.5cm) waste cotton fabric
- 3 x 9in (7.5 x 23cm) 11 count Aida fabric, in Cream
- Sewing thread
- Stranded cottons as in the colour key
- Thread organiser
- Two tapestry needles, size 24
- 3 x 9in (7.5 x 23cm) iron-on Vilene
- 22in (56cm) length of cotton lace edging
- Short length of 4mm Offray embroidery ribbon to make into a bow, shade Tropic 323 (or any toning ribbon)

## STORING THREAD ON AN ORGANISER (STEPS 1 – 2)

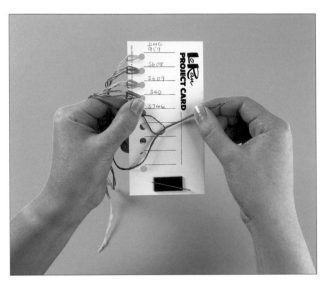

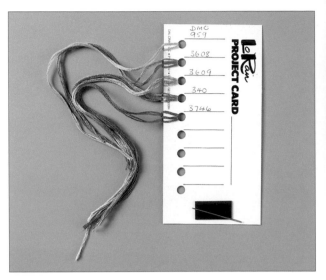

1 To prevent precious thread getting lost or tangled into an irretrievable mess, mount spare strands onto a thread organiser. To do this, fold the strands in half to form a loop, pass the loop through the hole in the organiser and pass the ends of the strands through the loop.

2 Write the thread number next to the hole it occupies; this is particularly important when working with similar shades of one colour. As you work, finish off each area of colour as it is completed and store left-over thread on the organiser until it is needed again.

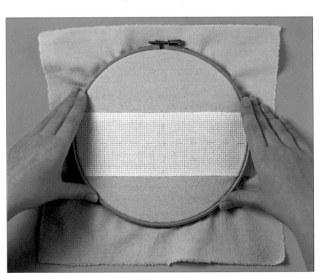

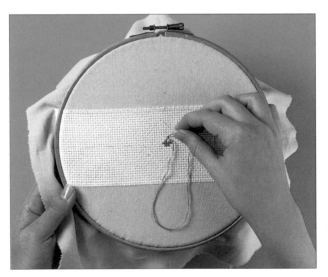

3 Stitch the strip of Aida embroidery fabric onto the waste fabric (pg19), and then mount the waste fabric into the hoop (pg17). Starting with the correct colour (as indicated by the central square on the chart), thread the needle (pg19).

4 Using a knotless start (pg24), begin stitching the heart at the centre of the design using the colour indicated on the chart. Follow the guidelines for working cross stitch described in Skill 1. (Refer also to The Golden Rules of Cross Stitch on pg117.)

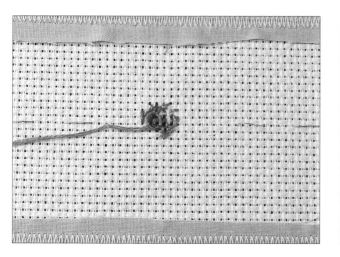

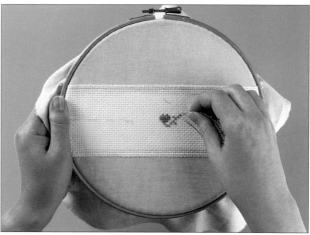

**5** When one area of colour is complete, join in another colour using the technique for adding a new thread (pg26), only this time using a different colour.

**6** When the central heart is complete, work the whole of the green trail – this establishes the positions of the rest of the hearts which can now be worked without complicated counting across bare fabric.

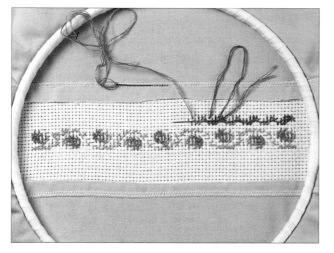

### Perfectionist's Corner

*As you work, twists will develop on your thread and if they are not removed the thread will twist tighter and tighter. This will not give good coverage of the fabric. To prevent this, allow the needle to dangle from the work regularly so it untwists, or turn the needle in your hand as you work to remove any twists.*

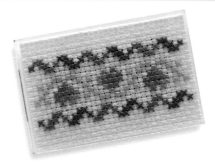

**7** To work the mauve border, thread one tapestry needle with light mauve and one with dark mauve. Work the first repeat with one needle and the second repeat with the other. On the back of the work, thread the first needle through the back of the stitches on the second repeat and bring the thread to the surface ready to work the third repeat. (You can bring thread from one area to another on the back of the work without finishing off and starting again only if it can be threaded through the back of existing stitches without showing on the surface.)

*Make a magnetic note holder from the same design (see chart pg36). Stitch on 11 count cream Aida and cover the back with iron-on Vilene. Cut the work to size and slip it into the mount. Some all-purpose adhesive on the back of the inside of the mount will prevent the work slipping.*

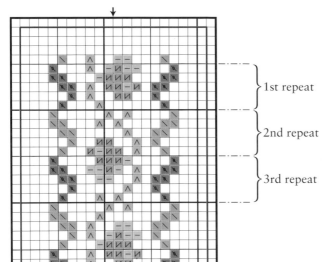

1st repeat

2nd repeat

3rd repeat

## MAKING UP THE BOOKMARK
### (STEPS 8 – 10)

**8** When the embroidery is finished, remove the fabric from the hoop, cut away and discard the waste fabric and remove the tacking threads from the embroidery. To stiffen the bookmark and hide the back of the work, back it with iron-on Vilene. Lay a white, fluffy, terry towel on a flat surface and put the embroidery face down onto it. Lay the iron-on Vilene over the back of the embroidery. Then following the manufacturer's instructions on the Vilene, press the work with an iron until it has bonded with the embroidery.

## BOOKMARK

### Colour Key

|  | DMC/Anchor |
|---|---|
| – – | 3609/85 |
| ⊠ ⊠ | 3746/118 |
| \ \ | 340/117 |
| И И | 3608/86 |
| ∧ ∧ | 959/186 |

—     Cutting line

☆     Middle point

## NOTES

Use three strands of stranded cotton to work all cross stitches.

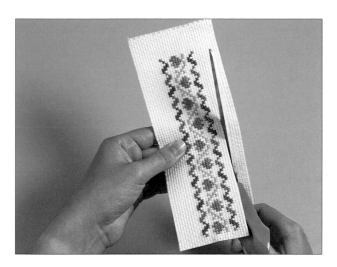

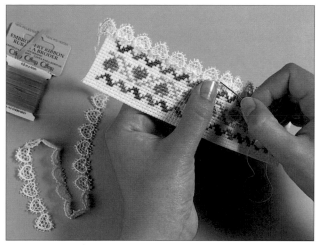

**9** Using your dressmaking scissors, cut the Vilene-backed embroidery along the cutting line marked on the chart. Carefully oversew the edges with a machine zig-zag stitch, or neatly by hand.

**10** Stitch a pretty, cotton lace edging around the edges – here hearts have been chosen to mirror the hearts in the design. Trim with a bow of toning ribbon (see Skill 1, Step 21, pg31).  Using embroidery ribbon to form a flat bow will not distort the pages of a book.

### TOWEL

*To cheer up a plain towel, a section of the bookmark design has been stitched and the colours changed to tone with the towel. (See pg32 for advice on choosing your own colours.) Following the chart on pg113, stitch the design on 1in (2.5cm) wide, white scalloped-edged Aida band. Stitch enough repeats of the design to fit the towel width, plus ½in (1.25cm) each end. Stitch the band to the towel, turning the ends in neatly on the back of the towel.*

# BACK STITCH LETTERING

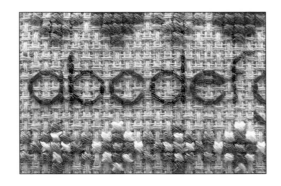

*ack stitch is so called because all the stitches worked on the front surface of the fabric are worked in a backwards direction, whilst those on the back of the work go forwards. This ensures that the slight backwards pull on each stitch gives it definition and neatness. Back stitch lettering is a useful addition to your cross stitch as it will allow you to work texts and personalise any future*

*work with names and dates. Finished pieces of work are more interesting if signed and dated. On larger pieces of stitching include the date of commencement as well as the date of completion to make sure that future generations appreciate your effort. When working back stitch for lettering to personalise a piece you will generally need to use two strands of stranded cotton in the needle.*

## A FIRST SAMPLER
*Finished Size: 3 x 4¼in (7.5 x 11cm)*

During the eighteenth and nineteenth centuries, cross stitch samplers were worked by school children as a classroom exercise. They provided a method of teaching the skills of needlework and also literacy, as alphabets

were generally included in the design. Some of the other traditional motifs commonly worked were houses, trees, animals, flowers and hearts. These elements are combined here to produce your first cross stitch sampler on a finer fabric and in colours which echo the soft tones of antique samplers. Also incorporated are letters and numbers worked in back stitch to give you practise in back stitch lettering.

*You Will Need*
- *7in (18cm) embroidery hoop*
- *11 x 11in (28 x 28cm) 14 count Rustico Aida fabric*
- *Stranded cottons as in the colour key*
- *Two tapestry needles, size 26*
- *Frame with an aperture 3¼ x 4½in (8 x 11.5cm)*

## A First Sampler

### *Colour Key*

DMC/Anchor
Cross stitch

| | |
|---|---|
| ·· | 781/309 |
| v v | Ecru/926 |
| □□ | 927/849 |
| ▬▬ | 3768/779 |
| + + | 502/876 |
| ×× | 833/907 |
| == | 3041/871 |
| ∷∷ | 356/1013 |

Backstitch

—  924/851
—  919/340

☆  Middle point

### NOTES

Use two strands of
stranded cotton to work all
cross stitches. Work back
stitches with two strands

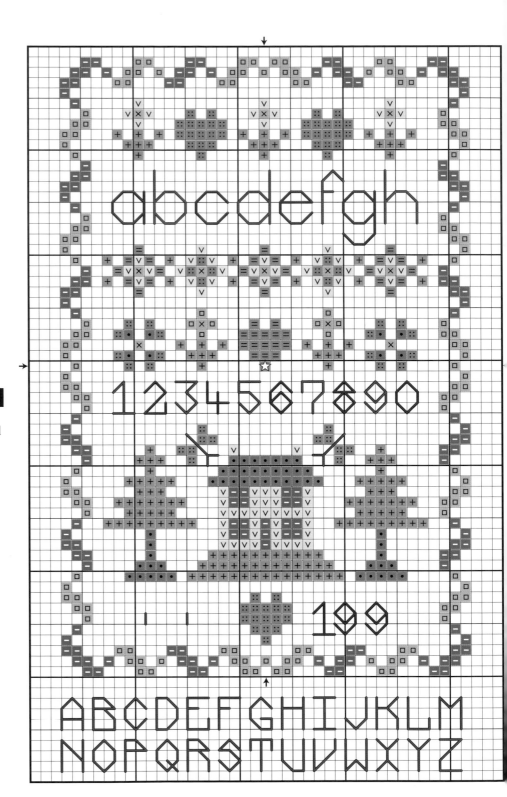

**1** Prepare the fabric for work (pg16) and mount it into the embroidery hoop (pg17).

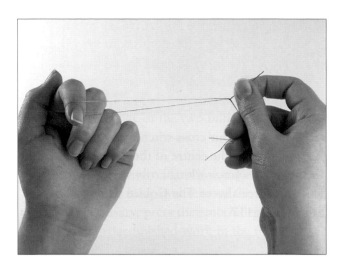

## LOOP STARTING METHOD
### (STEPS 2 – 5)

*This method can be used to start a thread neatly whenever you are using an even number of strands.*

**2** Cut a 20in (50cm) length of stranded cotton and separate one strand from the length. Double it to give two strands. Thread the two ends through the eye of the needle forming a loop which hangs from the needle.

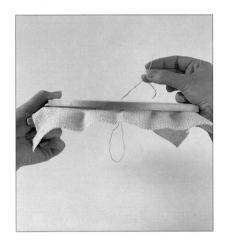

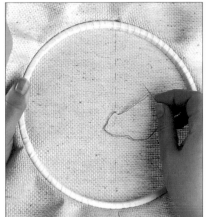

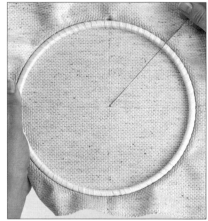

**3** Bring the needle to the surface of the fabric at the starting point leaving the loop on the back of the work.

**4** Take the needle to the back of the work to make the first half of the cross stitch and thread the needle through the loop.

**5** Tighten the thread and you have a neat, knotless start.

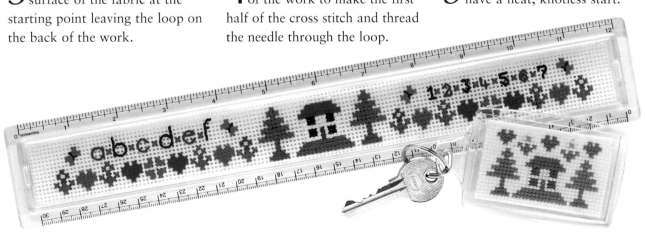

*Adapting designs is easy and addictive. See Ringing the Changes (pg108) for charts, instructions and ideas.*

# BACK STITCH OUTLINING

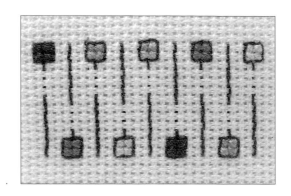

*𝒩ot only is back stitch used alongside cross stitch to form lettering, it is also used as an outliner and to add detail and definition to your work. Outlining gives the cross stitch a straight edge and a finished look, and is worked after the cross stitch has been completed. Usually less strands of cotton are used for outlining than are used for the cross stitch it complements.*

## CHATELAINE

*Finished Size: Chatelaine 1 x 46in (2.5 x 117cm); Pincushion 3 x 4in (7.5 x 10cm)*

Now you are ready to progress to working on Aida band, a finer fabric than you have used before. What better way to learn the skill of back stitch outlining than by making another stitcher's aid? No more hunting down the sides of the sofa for lost needles and scissors; a chatelaine which hangs around your neck will keep your pincushion and embroidery scissors always to hand.

If you are pressed for time, consider working just a few of the designs at each end of the band, enough to feel that you have mastered the technique. Eager beavers can stitch the whole lot.

### You Will Need
- *Small embroidery frame (optional)*
- *50in (127cm) Zweigart scalloped-edge Aida band, 1in (2.5cm) wide, in White with Sky edges*
- *Stranded cottons as in the colour key*
- *Tapestry needle, size 26*
- *50in (127cm) length of 15mm satin ribbon, in White*
- *White sewing thread*
- *7in (18cm) Zweigart scalloped-edge Aida band, 4in (10cm) wide, in White with Sky edges*
- *Small flexi-hoop*
- *Washable stuffing*
- *Sharp-pointed embroidery scissors*

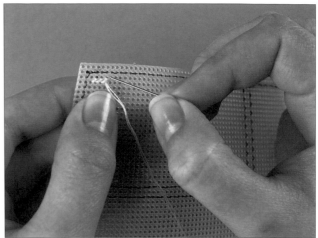

1 Tack the cutting lines shown on the chart to mark out the six pieces that make up the basket onto your sheet of plastic canvas. You should end up with two long sides, two short ends, one base and one handle.

2 Work with the plastic canvas in your hand and cross stitch exactly as if you were working on fabric. Starting with one of the long sides, and using the loop starting method (pg41), begin by stitching one space in from the cutting line.

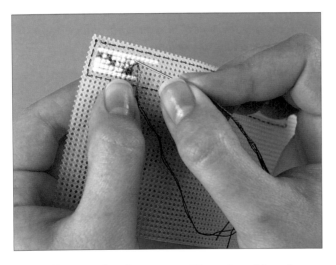

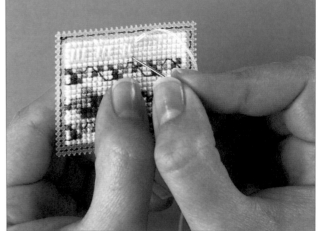

3 Following the chart on pg58, and making the colour changes as necessary, complete the cross stitching on all the six pieces of plastic canvas.

4 Work the vertical stitches that carry the ribbon using three strands of stranded cotton, in the positions marked on the chart.

## *Perfectionist's Corner*

*Perfectionists would not dream of cheating by not stitching the base of the basket because it is rarely, if ever, on view... would they?*

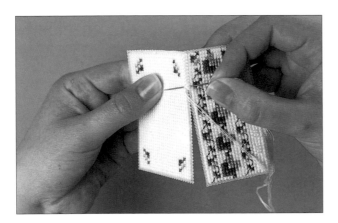

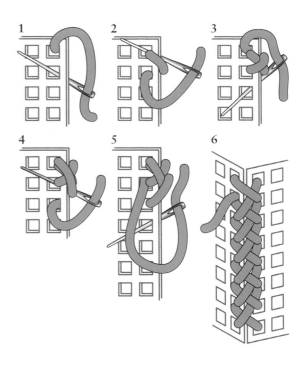

8 Join each of the long sides in turn to the base using the joining stitch shown right. This will give a decorative, plaited finish. Now join the short ends to the base to form a basket, again using the joining stitch. Finally, using the same stitch, work each vertical join at the corners from the base upwards.

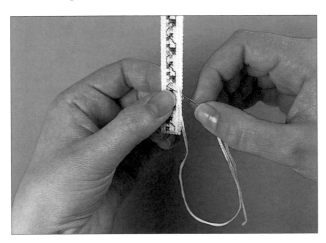

9 Work the edging stitch shown in the diagram below, all round the top of the basket and down each side of the handle.

10 Line the handle by gluing the appropriate piece of felt in place on the back of the work. Stitch the ends of the handle to the sides of the basket, on the inside.

11 Line the basket by gluing the other pieces of felt in their correct positions on the inside, so that the back of the work is covered.

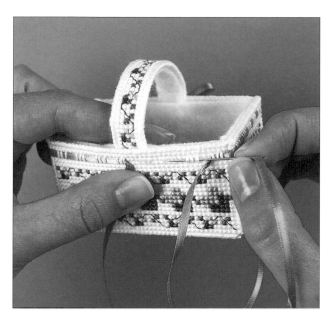

**12** Cut the ribbon in half and using the needle, thread one half at a time through the vertical carrying stitches so that the ends of the ribbon come out half-way round each side under the handle. Tie a bow on each side and trim the ends of the ribbon.

## MAKING UP THE PINCUSHION (STEPS 13 – 15)

**13** Using sewing thread, take a fine running stitch around the edge of the piece of toning cotton fabric.

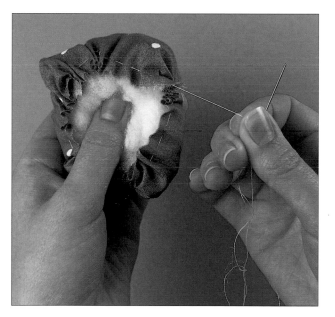

**14** Place a small amount of stuffing in the centre of the fabric, pull the running thread up around it to form a cushion and then tie off the thread securely.

**15** Push the cushion into the basket so that the raw and gathered edges of the fabric are hidden. Finally, place the decorative pearlised pins in the pincushion, ready for use.

# WORKING WITH PERFORATED PAPER

*erforated paper, sometimes known as stitching paper, enjoyed great popularity during the Victorian era. The vogue was to use the paper to stitch all manner of small items – bookmarks, needle cases, alphabets, as well as larger mottoes to frame and hang on the wall. In* spite of its apparent fragility it is quite durable, allowing the edges to be cut into any shape without fraying. The revival of interest in Victorian crafts means that supplies are now available again. It can be bought in many colours including gold and silver, and has a count of 14 holes to 1in (2.5cm).

## TREASURE BOX
*Finished Size: 1 x 2 x 2in (2.5 x 5 x 5cm)*

The ability to cut and manipulate perforated paper is exploited to the full in this project where a simple pattern is cut and folded into a treasure box, something which would be impossible if the design were stitched on fabric or plastic canvas. Use the box to hold a favourite piece of jewellery, a sentimental memento, or any small treasure. Alternatively, treat a friend to a gift box which conceals a special birthday surprise.

*You Will Need*
- *One sheet of perforated stitching paper, in Off-White*
- *Steel ruler*
- *Lead pencil*
- *Stranded cottons as in the colour key*
- *Tapestry needle, size 26*
- *Sharp paper-cutting scissors*
- *Craft knife*
- *Clear, all-purpose adhesive*
- *Paper-clips*

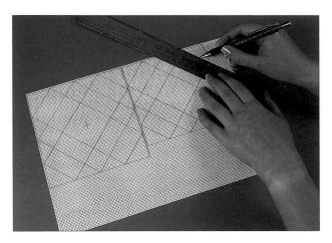

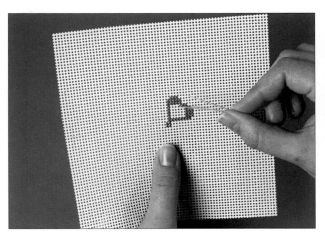

**1** Using the chart to guide you, mark the outline of the embroidered lid (opposite) and the unworked base of the box (below) on the wrong side of the perforated paper using a pencil and ruler. (The rougher side of the paper is the wrong side.) First, mark the outermost square, then the diagonal lines within. (Stitches are worked over the solid areas of paper between holes, so your pencil marks need to run along lines of holes.)

**2** Using the pencilled lines on the back of the work as a guide, start, with a knotless start (pg24), to stitch in the centre of the central diamond. Stitch the whole design, taking care not to form bulky lumps when you finish and start. (The smoother the work, the easier it will be to fold into an undistorted lid.) Plan your stitching route with great care, avoiding thread across the back of empty holes where it will be visible.

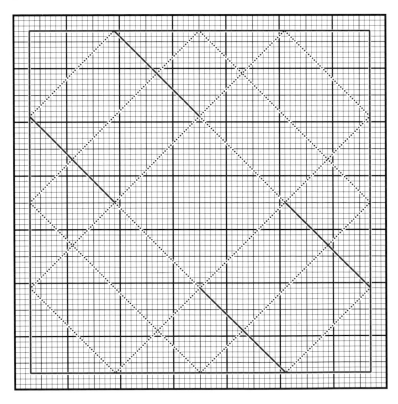

## Perfectionist's Corner

*The use of a hoop or frame is not necessary when working with perforated paper, but if the paper is mounted into an embroidery frame it suffers less from handling. Always ensure that your hands are clean and dry before handling perforated paper; hand cream can stain the paper and render it useless. Any small tears can be repaired invisibly on the back with clear adhesive tape. Apply the tape to the torn area, smooth it down over the tear to restore the surface and continue stitching through the tape.*

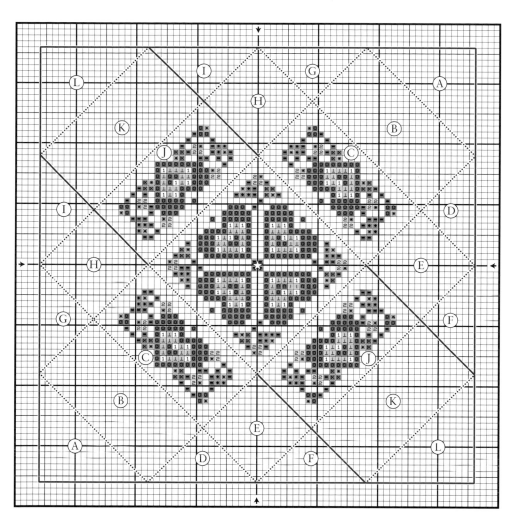

### TREASURE BOX

#### Colour Key

| | DMC/Anchor |
|---|---|
| | Cross stitch |
| 1 1 | Blanc/1 |
| 2 2 | Ecru/926 |
| ✖ ✖ | 518/1039 |
| 0 0 | 351/10 |
| ⊥ ⊥ | 353/6 |
| ▬ ▬ | 502/876 |
| ✳ ✳ | 676/891 |
| ◆ ◆ | 352/9 |

| | | |
|---|---|---|
| —— | | Cut along these lines |
| ........ | | Score along these lines |
| ☆ | | Middle point |

#### NOTES

Work all cross stitches with three strands of stranded cotton.

3 When the embroidery is complete, use sharp paper-cutting scissors to cut along the outer cutting line of the embroidered lid. Make the four diagonal cuts marked on the chart.

4 Placing your work on a cutting mat, score along the rest of the diagonal fold lines on the back, using a craft knife held against a steel ruler. Score lightly to avoid cutting right through the paper.

# WORKING WITH AIDA PLUS

*A*ida Plus is a modern fabric which has many of the useful properties of perforated paper, but none of its weaknesses. You can cut it, trim it and shape it without any unravelling, fraying or splitting and, unlike perforated paper, it is hand-washable and will not tear. As this project demonstrates, it even allows you to weave with

it. This would be difficult with other fabric which would fray, or with perforated paper which might tear. 14 count Aida Plus is available in 9 x 12in (23 x 30.5cm) sheets, in a variety of colours. The fabric has a treated backing which prevents distortion, so no hoop or frame is necessary.

## CHRISTMAS HEART-SHAPED BASKETS
*Finished Size: 3½ x 3½in (9 x 9cm)*

Deck your Christmas tree with cross stitched baskets filled with sweets or other goodies. A basket can be stitched in an evening and the weaving takes only a few minutes. For variety, you could try combining different colours, for example green with red, or red with white. Pink with white, or pale blue with white with toning cross stitch and frothy lace trimmings could make a romantic gift for Valentine's Day.

### You Will Need
- One sheet 14 count Aida Plus fabric, in Emerald Green (4718)
- One sheet 14 count Aida Plus fabric, in White (4700) or Red (4716)
- Stranded cottons as in the colour key
- Tapestry needle, size 26
- Sharp, fine-pointed scissors
- Scraps of braid, lace, ribbon and cord
- Clear, all-purpose adhesive

### NAPKIN HOLDER
*This napkin holder uses the motifs from the main project. Work on white perforated paper, back with pretty wrapping paper, cut to size and place in the mount (chart, pg114).*

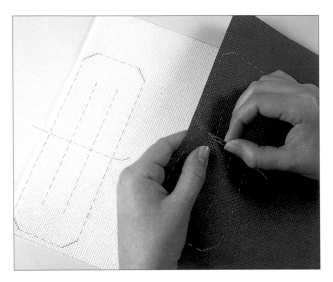

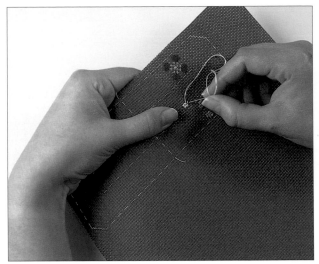

1 On the white Aida Plus fabric, tack the outline of the pattern, shown on the chart as the cutting line. Mark the two central cutting lines in the same way. The tacking threads will guide you to the correct position for the stitching, and when work is complete, show you where to cut the fabric. Mark the green Aida Plus fabric in the same way.

2 Take the green Aida Plus fabric and using the loop starting method (pg41), work all the cross stitches exactly as you would on any other Aida fabric, following all The Golden Rules of Cross Stitch (pg117). The white Aida Plus remains unstitched and is used for the weaving (Steps 7–9, pgs72–3).

## MAKING UP THE BASKETS (STEPS 3 – 6)

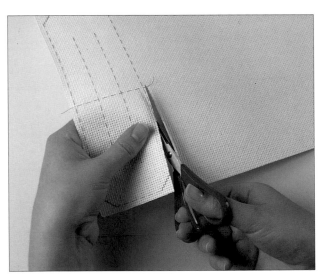

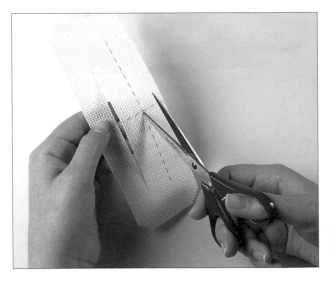

3 Using sharp, fine-pointed scissors cut along the outer cutting line of the white Aida Plus fabric.

4 Cut along the two central cutting lines, using the fine points of the scissors to pierce the fabric at the start of each cut. Remove any tacking threads which remain.

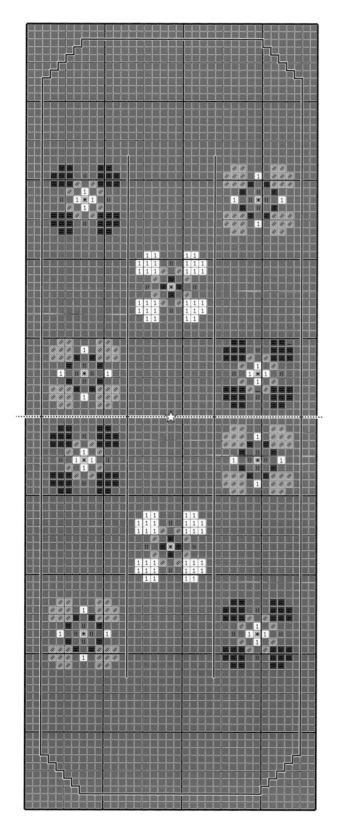

**5** Repeat Steps 3 and 4 with the stitched piece of green Aida Plus.

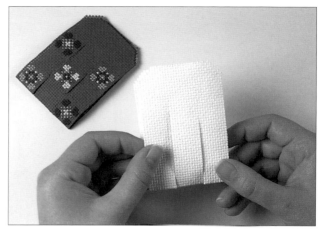

**6** Carefully fold each of the Aida Plus pieces in half, wrong sides together, along the fold line marked on the chart.

## CHRISTMAS HEART-SHAPED BASKETS

### Colour Key

|  | DMC/Anchor |
|---|---|
|  | Cross stitch |
| 1 1 | Blanc/1 |
| II II | 793/176 |
| ▬ ▬ | 666/335 |
| ▬ | Background green fabric |
| ⁄ ⁄ | 703/238 |
| * * | 726/295 |
| — | Cutting lines |
| ....... | Folding line |
| ☆ | Middle point |

**NOTES**

Work all cross stitches with two strands of stranded cotton.

## PORCELAIN BOWL & NAPKIN HOLDER

*A basket motif has been used for these items. The 1¼in (3cm) bowl lid is worked on cream 22 count Zweigart Oslo Hardanger with soft colours. The napkin holder is a pastel version of the one on pg68. (For charts see pg114.)*

## WEAVING THE BASKET (STEPS 7 – 9)

*Holding the green fabric in your right hand and the white in your left, weave the two into a basket following the instructions and photographic sequence described below.*

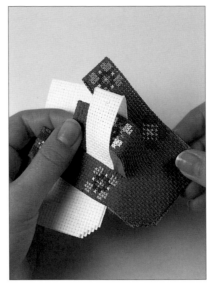

7 *First Row* (a) Weave the 1st white loop through the centre of the 1st green loop.

(b) Weave the 2nd green loop through the centre of the 1st white loop.

(c) Weave the 1st white loop through the centre of the 3rd green loop.

8 *Second Row* (a) Weave the 1st green loop through the centre of the 2nd white loop.

(b) Weave the 2nd white loop through the centre of the 2nd green loop.

(c) Weave the 3rd green loop through the centre of the 2nd white loop.

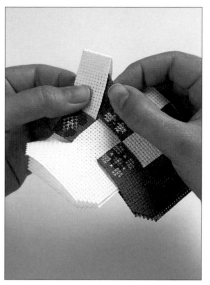

**9** *Third Row* (a) Weave the 3rd white loop through the centre of the 1st green loop.

(b) Weave the 2nd green loop through the centre of the 3rd white loop.

(c) Weave the 3rd white loop through the centre of the 3rd green loop to complete the weaving.

**10** Trim the finished basket by gluing lace or braid to it, using the stitched sample pictured on pg69 as a guide. Make a hanger by adding a loop of ribbon or cord, attaching one end to the centre front of the basket, and the other to the centre back. Trim the centre front and back with a small bow of toning ribbon. Fill with sweets or small goodies and hang on the Christmas tree.

## Perfectionist's Corner

*The properties of Aida Plus make it particularly suitable for three-dimensional projects. If you are working an Aida Plus project where the back of your work is going to be on view you may wish to cover the back of the stitching. A second piece of Aida Plus can be ironed onto the back of your stitched work to line and stiffen it. Place both pieces of Aida Plus fabric wrong sides together, with the embroidery face down on a thick, white terry towel. Cover with a pressing cloth and iron with a medium heat until the fabrics are bonded. Allow to cool flat, then check the bond and if necessary repeat the ironing process until a satisfactory bond is achieved. When the pieces are securely fused they can be trimmed to the desired shape.*

# USING WASTE CANVAS

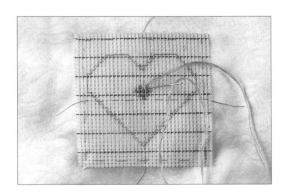

*A*ll the fabrics used so far in this book have been specially designed for counted thread embroidery, but the good news is that you are not limited to working only on specialist fabrics. Cross stitch can be worked on any fabric which can be pierced with a needle if waste canvas is first applied to the surface of that fabric. The waste canvas provides the missing holes which act as guidelines for the stitching. It is available in a variety of counts and consists of threads which are woven into an even grid which is held rigidly in place with starch. When work is complete, the waste canvas threads are removed, leaving the stitched design on the surface of your chosen fabric.

## CHRISTENING ROBE
*Finished Size of Heart: 2 x 1¾in (5 x 4.5cm)*

Waste canvas opens up the possibility of stitching on all manner of garments, and here a christening robe has been beautifully embellished with a floral heart cross stitch design. The more adventurous could add a name and date using back stitch outlining (see Skill 3). An alternative patchwork heart design suitable for working on children's everyday clothes is shown on pg111 in Ringing the Changes, and is charted on pg113.

*You Will Need*
- *Christening robe with a yoke*
- *2½ x 2½in (6.5 x 6.5cm) 14 count waste canvas*
- *Embroidery hoop (optional)*
- *Stranded cottons as in the colour key*
- *Tapestry needle, size 26 (or crewel needle)*
- *Small amount of cotton wool*
- *Tweezers*
- *White sewing thread*
- *Trimmings to suit the robe (ribbon, roses, beads)*

*HEART-SHAPED PORCELAIN BOWL*
*Embroidered on cream 14 count Aida, the colours have been altered to match a 3½in (9cm) porcelain bowl (chart pg113).*

**1** Carefully measure out and mark the centre of the yoke on the christening robe using two intersecting lines of tacking thread.

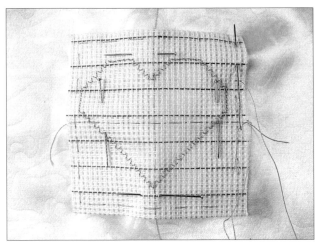

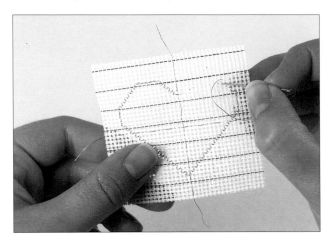

**2** Using the chart to guide you, tack the outline of the heart onto the waste canvas.

**3** Position the waste canvas on the yoke so that the outline of the heart is in the correct position and then tack the waste canvas to the yoke. Mount the waste canvas and yoke into an embroidery hoop, if possible (pg17).

## CHRISTENING ROBE

### Colour Key

DMC/Anchor
Cross stitch

| | |
|---|---|
| ⌐⌐ | 504/1042 |
| ✗✗ | 927/848 |
| ++ | 225/1026 |
| ▼▼ | 677/886 |
| ♥♥ | 778/968 |
| ◇◇ | 3743/869 |

— Tacking thread outline

☆ Middle point

### NOTES

Work all cross stitches with three strands of stranded cotton. Use a tapestry needle if it will pierce the fabric of the robe. If not, use a crewel needle, but take care not to split or catch the waste canvas threads as this will lead to difficulties when you come to withdraw the threads.

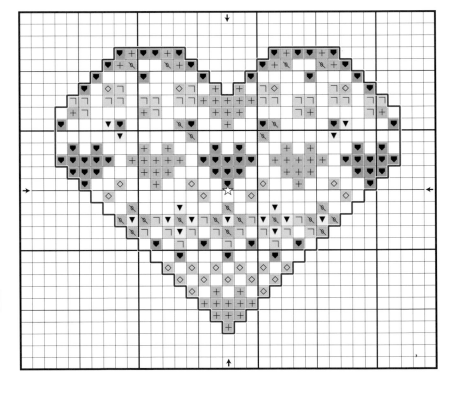

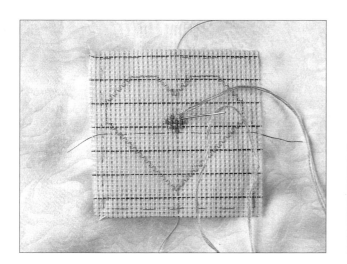

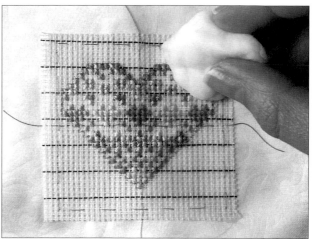

4 Using a knotless start (pg24) and beginning with the small pink heart in the centre of the design, work the cross stitch pattern, but make sure that the stitches go through both the waste canvas *and* the fabric of the robe.

5 When the embroidery is complete, dampen a pad of cotton wool with clean water and dab it all over the waste canvas to moisten it and thus soften the starch. This will make the threads of the canvas go limp so they are easier to remove.

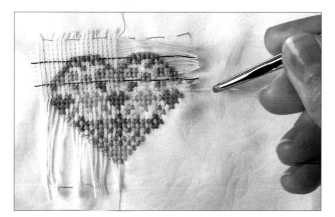

6 Using tweezers, gently pull out the threads of the waste canvas one by one, removing the tacking threads as you come to them. Allow the robe to dry.

7 Using white sewing thread, trim the robe with lace, ribbon, beads and trimmings of your choice to tone with the embroidery.

## *Perfectionist's Corner*

Because you are not working on an Aida or evenweave fabric you will have to form the holes for the stitches yourself, using the holes in the waste canvas as guides. The needle must pierce the exact centre of each hole or the threads will be difficult to remove later. Where two or more stitches share the same hole, check they enter or emerge through the same hole. Working on waste canvas seems simple but it is easy to end up with an untidy result, so work with particular care.

# WORKING WITH EVENWEAVE FABRIC

*U*nlike canvas work, where the whole of the canvas is covered with stitches which obscure the canvas, in cross stitch embroidery the background of a design is not worked. Consequently the embroidery fabric is on show and forms part of the finished work. Aida fabrics consist of blocks which form a regular, square pattern, but with evenweave fabrics, such as linen,

you get a smoother, less obtrusive background to your stitching. Up till now you have worked the cross stitch over one block: now you will be working over two threads instead, so a thread count of 20 will produce 10 cross stitches to 1in (2.5cm). You will soon get accustomed to counting pairs of threads, rather than blocks as you did with Aida fabrics.

# WEDDING PICTURE
### Finished Size: 4¼ x 8in (11 x 20cm)

For a first attempt at working on evenweave fabric, a cotton/viscose mix has been chosen with a low thread count so it will be easy to see the holes and count the pairs of threads. The chosen theme is a wedding, where the initials of your choice can be added from the alphabet provided on pg83. The wedding bells will give you your first experience of metal thread cross stitch.

**You Will Need**
- 10in (25.5cm) embroidery hoop
- 14 x 14in (35.5 x 35.5cm) 20 count Zweigart Bellana evenweave fabric, in Antique White
- Stranded cottons as in the colour key
- DMC Light Silver thread
- Tapestry needle, size 24

- Small bow of white ribbon, trimmed with a pearl bead
- Frame of your choice, with aperture larger than 4¼ x 8in (11 x 20cm)

1 Prepare the fabric with tacking thread (pg16–17) and mount it into the hoop as usual. Using a knotless start (pg24), bring the needle to the front of the work ready to work the first stitch near the centre of the design.

*This lovely wedding card has been worked on a high count fabric – see pg112 for making up instructions.*

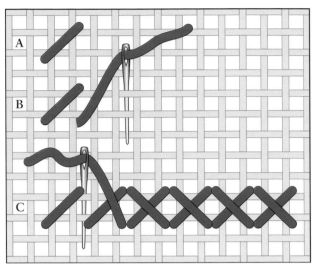

2 Put the needle into the fabric two threads to the right and two threads up, as shown in diagram A above. Bring the needle to the surface again two threads below as shown in diagram B above. Continue this sequence to the end of the row. Once at the end of the row, return, crossing each stitch and using the same holes as before so that all cross stitches 'hold hands' as shown in diagram C above.

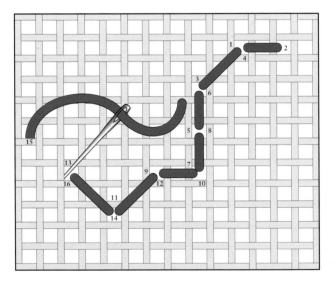

3 When the cross stitching is complete, work the back stitch outlining over two threads as shown in the diagram above. (See Skill 4 to recap back stitch outlining and also Perfectionist's Corner on pg82.)

## WEDDING PICTURE

### Colour Key

DMC/Anchor
Cross stitch

| | |
|---|---|
| – – | Blanc/1 |
| I I | 993/186 |
| 1 1 | 414/235 |
| 2 2 | 415/398 |
| 3 3 | 434/310 |
| 4 4 | 744/301 |
| 5 5 | 3713/1020 |
| 6 6 | 3716/25 |
| 7 7 | 3761/928 |
| ● | 413/236 |
| 9 9 | DMC light silver thread |

Backstitch

413/236
962/75
518/1039

— Position initials here
....... Position date here

### NOTES

Work all cross stitches with three strands of stranded cotton. Use one strand for back stitch outlining, two strands for initials and the date. Use one strand to work the French knots. Use two strands of DMC Light Silver thread to work the bells.

## Perfectionist's Corner

*Take care when back stitching because your route may take the thread across the back of bare fabric and with evenweave fabric this may show through an empty hole. To work the stitch illustrated in diagram 1, bring the needle out at point 'b', in at 'a' and out again at 'c'. The stitch on the back of the work may show through hole 'd'. To correct this, put the needle in again at 'b'. On the back of the work, slip the needle under the back stitch which lies between 'a' and 'c', as shown in diagram 2 and bring the needle to the front of the work at 'e'. The tension on the thread between 'b' and 'e' will pull the stitch into place along the edge of the embroidery at the back of the work, shown in diagram 3.*

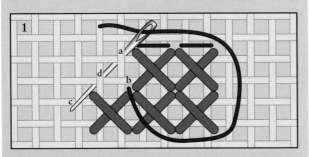

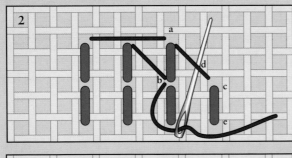

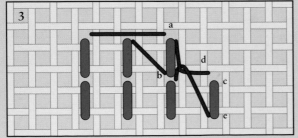

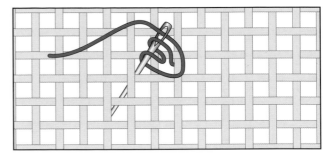

**4** Work the French knots over one thread as shown in the diagram above. (See Skill 5 to recap French knots.)

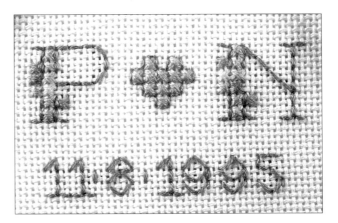

**5** Work the wedding date and the initials of the bride and groom as indicated on the chart on pg81, positioning them so there are four bare threads (two squares on the chart) on either side of the heart. (See Skill 3 to recap back stitch lettering.)

**6** Work the bells with silver thread. Metal thread often appears to have a mind of its own; it is springier than stranded cotton and less easy to handle so cut shorter lengths of thread than usual to avoid tangling and fraying. This design requires two strands of silver thread to work the bells, but it is easier to work with one strand in the needle and work each stitch twice as you go, building up to a total of two strands. This makes the metal thread easier to control and gives a better finish.

**7** Trim the silver bells with a bow of ribbon and frame the finished work as preferred.

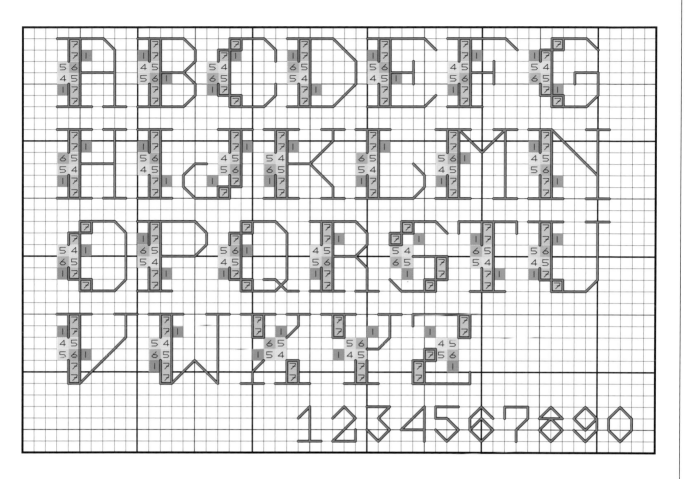

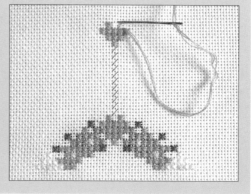

## ALPHABET & NUMBERS

### Colour Key

DMC/Anchor
Cross stitch

| | | |
|---|---|---|
| 1 1 | 993/186 |
| 4 4 | 744/301 |
| 5 5 | 3713/1020 |
| 6 6 | 3716/25 |
| 7 7 | 3761/928 |

Backstitch
— 992/187

## NOTES

Work all cross stitches with three strands of stranded cotton. Use one strand for back stitch outlining, two strands for initials and the date.

## *Perfectionist's Corner*

*Counting across bare evenweave fabric can be tricky when you are finding the starting position of another part of the design. Thread a needle with some light-coloured tacking thread and work the first half of a cross stitch to correspond with each blank square on the chart. Continue across the bare fabric until you reach the new starting position. Check carefully that the number of half crosses matches exactly the number of blank squares on the chart. Start to cross stitch the design in the correct position and then remove the tacking thread stitches.*

# INTRODUCING
# THREE-QUARTER CROSS STITCH

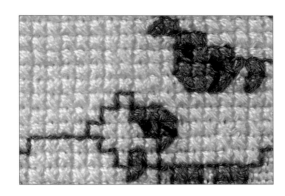

*N*ow that you have graduated onto evenweave
fabric it is possible to produce this fractional
stitch which, when combined with full cross stitch, is
used to produce more detail and the illusion of
curves in very small designs. Compare the hearts on this
design with the heart in the previous chapter and
you will see that the 'stepped' effect has been replaced
with a more rounded appearance.

# BIRTH ANNOUNCEMENT CARD
*Finished Size: 2½ x 4¼in (6.5 x 10.75cm)*

Announce a birth, or welcome a
new baby with this design which
consists mainly of full cross
stitches but which features for
the first time the occasional
three-quarter cross stitch. Pastel
colours have been used for this
design, so you may like to
consider stitching with DMC
Flower thread for an even softer
effect.

*You Will Need*
- *6in (15cm) embroidery hoop*
- *10 x 10in (25.5 x 25.5cm)
  28 count Jobelan evenweave
  fabric, in White*
- *Stranded cottons or DMC
  Flower thread as in the
  colour key*
- *Tapestry needle, size 26*
- *DMC Chelsea Studio Card
  mount with a 2¾ x 4⅜in
  (7 x 11cm) aperture*

- *Dress-making scissors*
- *Paper-cutting scissors or craft
  knife and metal ruler*
- *Double-sided adhesive tape*
- *Small cardboard box*
- *Scrap paper*
- *Spray Mount adhesive*
- *Ribbon to trim card*

Opposite *This design can also be
made up into a wall hanging, for
full instructions see pg 112.*

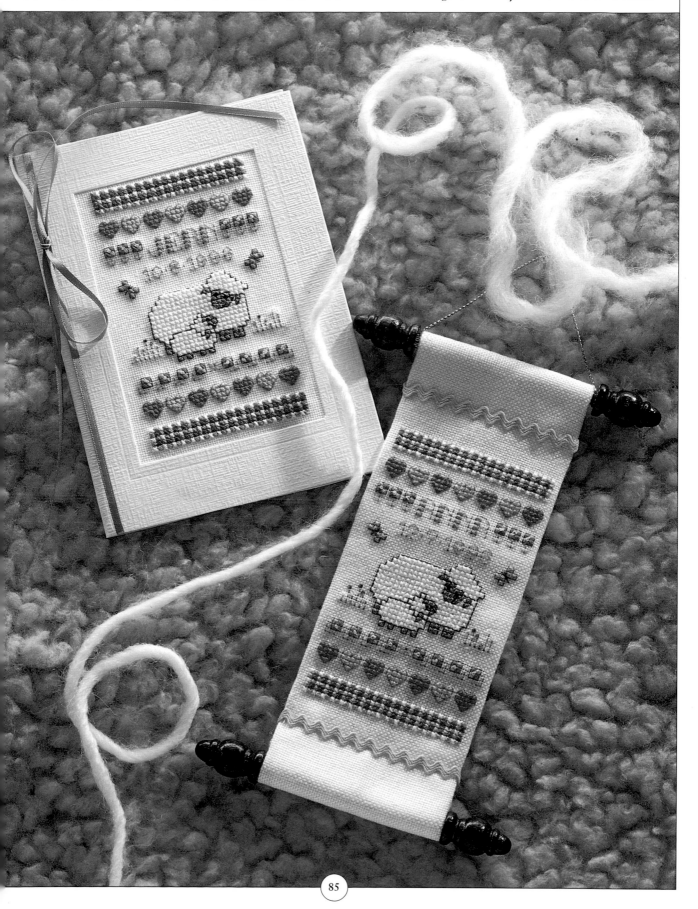

## THREE-QUARTER CROSS STITCH

Because stitches on evenweave fabrics are worked over two threads you now have a total of nine holes at your disposal in the space of one full cross stitch (see diagram A, below). The central hole (no. 5), non-existent on an Aida block, makes it possible to work a three-quarter cross stitch. Full cross stitch forms a square shape and three-quarter cross stitch forms a right-angled triangle (see diagrams B and C, below).

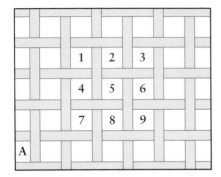

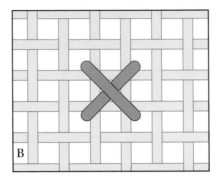

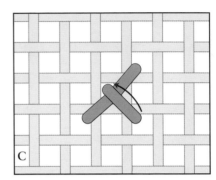

1 Prepare the fabric and mount it into a hoop (pg16–17). Following the chart and using the loop starting method (pg41), work the cross stitches. A square shape on the chart indicates a full cross stitch. A symbol in a right-angled triangle indicates that you should work a three-quarter stitch as follows. Work the first half of the cross stitch as usual in the direction indicated by the slope on the triangle symbol on the chart (the diagrams below illustrate how the chart symbols translate into stitches). Work the second stitch over the top of the first stitch and bring the needle down into the centre hole, as shown above right. (This will sometimes break the Golden Rule of always having the top stitch lying in the same direction, but it is necessary that the top stitch neatly anchors the bottom one by passing over the top of it, as shown in the detail photograph below.)

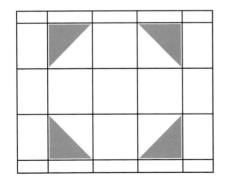

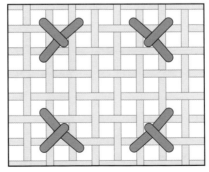

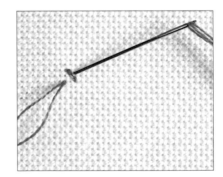

*Perfectionist's Corner*

*When working three-quarter cross stitches, do not pull the first stitch tight before working the quarter stitch as this will obscure the hole into which you work the quarter stitch. Leave the first stitch slack, exposing the central hole, insert the needle into the central hole and stop. Now pull the first stitch tight and complete the second stitch as normal.*

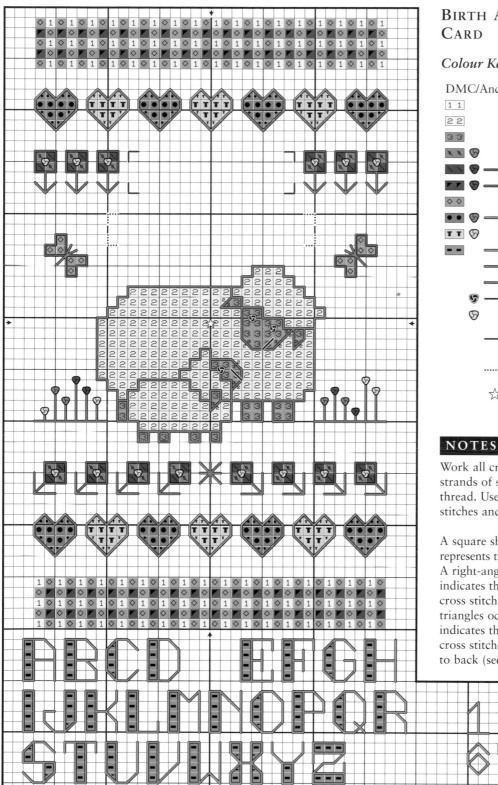

## BIRTH ANNOUNCEMENT CARD

### *Colour Key*

DMC/Anchor/Flower Thread

| | |
|---|---|
| 1  1 | Blanc/1/Blanc |
| 2  2 | 746/275/Ecru |
| 3  3 | 414/235/2414 |
| | 809/130/2799 |
| | 798/131/2798 |
| | 552/99/2532 |
| | 554/96/2210 |
| | 603/62/2899 |
| T  T | 605/50/2776 |
| -  - | 993/186/2952 |
| | 992/187/2956 |
| | 413/236/2413 |
| | 310/403/2310 |
| | 744/301/2743 |

| | |
|---|---|
| ——— | Position name or initials here |
| ........ | Position date here |
| ☆ | Middle point |

### NOTES

Work all cross stitches with two strands of stranded cotton or Flower thread. Use one strand to work back stitches and French knots.

A square shape on the chart represents the use of a full cross stitch. A right-angled triangle on the chart indicates the use of a three-quarter cross stitch. Two right-angled triangles occupying the same square indicates that two three-quarter cross stitches should be worked back to back (see Step 3, pg88).

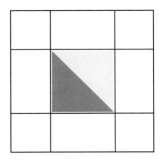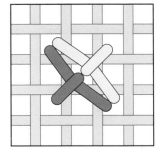

2 When working the hearts (above) you will find that they include the three-quarter cross stitch in all of its four possible positions (see diagram below).

3 Where two three-quarter stitches occupy the space of a full cross stitch they must be worked back to back, sharing the central hole. This occurs when you work the ears and noses on the sheep.

4 Work the French knot 'flowers'. (See Skill 5 to recap French knots.) Space has been left on the chart so that you can personalise your work with a short name or initials and a date, using the alphabet and numbers provided. (See Skill 3 to recap back stitch lettering.)

## MOUNTING EMBROIDERY IN A CARD (STEPS 5 – 10)

*When the embroidery is complete you are ready to mount the work into a card. Card mounts are readily available in an enormous variety of colours, shapes and sizes with pre-cut apertures for your finished work.*

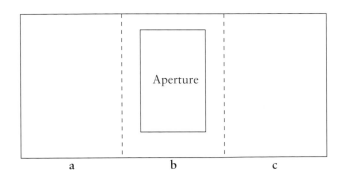

5 Establish which is the top and which is the bottom of the card. To do this look at section 'b' in the diagram, left. At the top of the card the border around the aperture is narrower than the border at the bottom of the card.

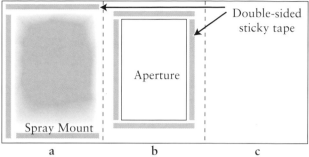

Double-sided sticky tape

Aperture

Spray Mount

a      b      c

6 Check that the card folds shut without gaping. If necessary cut a thin sliver of card off section 'a' to make it shut correctly. Use paper-cutting scissors for this, or better still a sharp craft knife held against a steel ruler if you have them. When using a craft knife protect the surface on which you are cutting with several layers of cardboard or a cutting mat.

8 Lay the embroidery face up on a flat surface. Remove the backing strips from the double-sided adhesive tape. Hold the card face up and position the aperture around the embroidery, checking that the work is straight and central and pressing the embroidery onto the adhesive tape. Do not worry if you do not get it right first time as the double-sided adhesive tape will allow you to have several attempts.

7 Using dressmaking scissors, trim the embroidery to fit the aperture, leaving ½in (1.25cm) spare fabric all round. Using paper-cutting scissors, cut lengths of double-sided adhesive tape to fit around the aperture and section 'a' (see diagram above). On the inside of the card stick the lengths of double-sided adhesive tape in the positions shown.

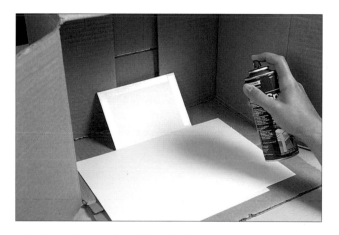

9 Place the card, right-side down, in a small grocery carton, mask off sections 'b' and 'c' with scrap paper and spray a squirt of Spray Mount onto section 'a'. The grocery carton and scrap paper will stop the adhesive going where it is not wanted and the Spray Mount will give the embroidery a sticky surface onto which to cling without rippling.

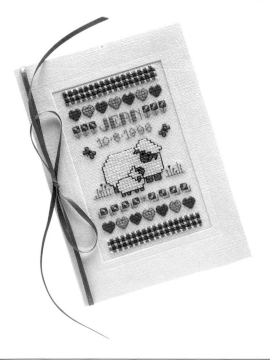

10 Fold section 'a' over section 'b', stroke down firmly and write your message on section 'c'. Trim with a length of fine ribbon tied around the card.

# ADVANCED
# THREE-QUARTER CROSS STITCH

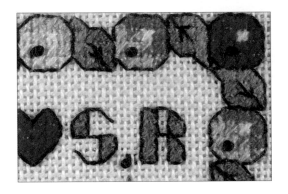

*Extensive use of three-quarter cross stitch in all its forms is used in this design, offering you plenty of practise in fractional stitching. This chapter also introduces you to tweeding, a subtle method of shading, where two different colours of stranded cotton are used together in the needle.*

# FAMILY TREE
*Finished Size: 4¾ x 4¾in (12 x 12cm)*

Three generations are represented on this family tree which is adaptable to suit everybody's circumstances. Simply change the initials to suit

the family history using the alphabet supplied. Photocopy the design and draw the required initials in the spaces on the chart. Place the grandparents' initials on the top line, the parents' on the second, and the child's initials on the bottom line. The border is composed of apples at various stages of maturity to reflect the different ages pictured on the family tree.

*You Will Need*
- *8in (20cm) embroidery hoop*
- *12 x 12in (30.5 x 30.5cm) Zweigart 27 count Linda evenweave fabric, in Antique White (101)*
- *Stranded cottons as in the colour key*
- *Tapestry needle, size 26*
- *Jewellery jump rings (optional)*

Place an initial either side of the French knots

1 Prepare the fabric for work (pg16) and mount into the hoop (pg17). Using the loop starting method (pg41), stitch over two threads of the fabric. Work the full and the three-quarter stitches first, then the back stitches and French knots.

## TWEEDING (STEPS 2 – 4)

The ripening apples in the border are worked with two shades of stranded cotton. Where orange, for example, changes to yellow a row of 'tweeding' is worked to soften the transition and give a more natural effect. This is achieved quite simply by working the stitches with one strand of orange thread and one strand of yellow thread in the needle. The rest of the two-toned apples are worked in the same way, using the shades given in the colour key.

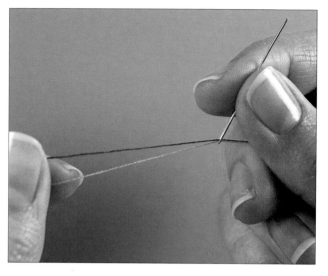

2 Thread the needle with two different colour threads.

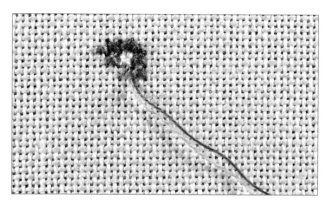

3 Work full and three-quarter cross stitches with the mixed colour thread (see Perfectionist's Corner, pg94).

4 Finish stitching the two-tone apple and carefully outline it in back stitch. (See Skill 4 to recap backstitch outlining.)

## FAMILY TREE

### Colour Key

| DMC/Anchor | | |
|---|---|---|
| Cross stitch | | |
| ■ 300/352 | ⑨⑨ 445/288 | 1 strand each of: |
| ①① Blanc/1 | ‖‖ 809/130 | ⊞⊞ 742/303 + 946/332 |
| ②② 746/275 | ■ 498/1005 | ◤◤ 704/256 + 445/288 |
| ⑤⑤ 946/332 | ⤢⤢ 318/399 | ✳✳ 445/288 + 742/303 |
| ⑥⑥ 948/6 | ◢◢ 797/132 | |
| ⑦⑦ 754/8 | ▲▲ 700/228 | Backstitch    French knot |
| ⑧⑧ 742/303 | ▬▬ 702/226 | —— 310/403   ❧ 310/403 |
| | ◪◪ 704/256 | —— 498/1005 |
| | ◖◖ 310/403 | —— 797/132   ☆ Middle point |

**NOTES**

Work all cross stitches with two strands of stranded cotton. Use one strand for back stitches and French knots.

## *Perfectionist's Corner*

In order to achieve the best coverage of the fabric possible when working with two strands of cotton, try a technique called 'railroading'. Before inserting your needle into the hole in the fabric, separate the two strands of cotton coming from the previous hole and pass the needle between the two strands as it enters the next hole. This serves to separate the strands, remove any twists from them and ensures that they lie neatly side by side.

## DEPICTING CHARACTER DETAILS

5 The people portrayed at the bottom of the design can be altered to look more like the actual people they represent. Height, hair colour and style, and clothing can all be altered as necessary, and jewellery jump rings can be stitched to faces for spectacle wearers. If you doubt your ability to alter the characters yourself and you throw up your hands in horror at the thought of drawing, consult my other books for help (pg118). There you will find all manner of clothing, footwear, hairstyles,

hats and other ideas which are interchangeable with those in this design, together with instructions for creating your own unique characters.

6 When the embroidery is complete, remove from the hoop and take out tacking threads. Press if necessary (pg30). Frame according to your choice.

# WORKING WITH SILK GAUZE

*T*his chapter is for those of you who think that small is beautiful as working with silk gauze gives stitchers the opportunity to work on a very tiny scale. Silk gauze, an even-count mono canvas made with raw silk fibres, is ideal for jewellery, doll's house projects and miniature framed pictures. It holds its shape whilst work is in progress, so no hoop is required, and it will not fray or need stretching after work is completed. It can be purchased in rolls if you plan to do a lot of this work, or in small squares which are conveniently mounted into a cardboard frame. You do need to be able to see the holes clearly if you are going to enjoy working on silk gauze and there are many aids on the market to help – from spectacles to special magnifiers.

## ZODIAC JEWELLERY
*Finished Size: 1¼ x 1in (3 x 2.5cm)*

Why not stitch your own birth sign or treat a friend to a very special birthday present?

The silk gauze chosen for your first attempt has 32 holes to 1in (2.5cm). Much finer silk gauze is available, and for more ambitious later efforts try working on a 50 count. Once you have adjusted to the small scale of the work you should find that working on silk gauze is as simple as working on Aida fabric. Each stitch is worked over one thread of the gauze.

Madeira silk embroidery floss has been chosen to work the Zodiac designs as one strand of the floss is just the right thickness to give good coverage of the gauze. Balger blending filament was chosen to work the gold stars because it is the 'twinkliest' gold thread available.

### You Will Need
• One 3½in (9cm) square of 32 count silk gauze (sufficient to work four designs)
• Madeira silk embroidery floss, Black and White
• Kreinik Metallics Balger blending filament Gold (002)
• Two tapestry needles, size 26
• Framecraft (GX2) oval gilt-plated jewellery mount, 1½ x 1⅛in (36 x 27mm)
• Gilt-plated chain for pendant or bow for fob brooch
• Spray Mount adhesive

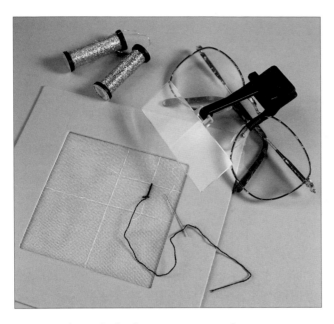

*A magnifier which clips onto spectacles is a great help with fine work.*

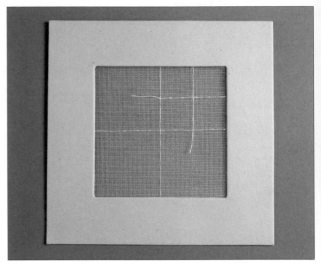

1 Start by dividing your square of silk gauze into four equal squares using tacking threads. Next subdivide one of the squares into four using tacking thread to find the centre of the square (pg17).

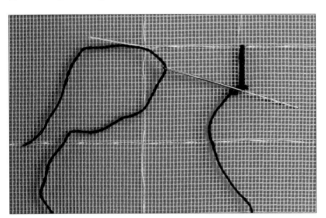

2 Thread one needle with one strand of black floss, and the other needle with one strand of white floss. Starting with a knotless start (pg24), work the design in the centre of the square, using all the usual techniques for starting, cross stitching and finishing. Work all stitches over one thread of the gauze.

4 Choose with great care the route that your cross stitch takes. Because the gauze is so transparent, never carry the thread over a part of the design which is not solidly stitched.

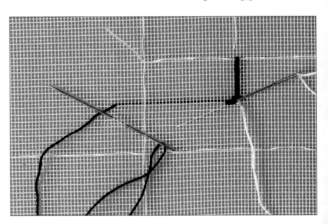

3 When you come to a white stitch, work it immediately alongside the black stitch, as you will not be able to see the gaps to fill in the white stitches later. Thus you will have two needles in use in the areas where there are white stitches. Keep the thread which is not working tucked to one side on the back of the gauze, out of the way until needed.

Opposite *The charted Zodiac designs on pg100–101 provide a perfect introduction to working with silk gauze; but they can just as easily be worked on Aida fabric too. See pg99 for details.*

# ORNAMENTED CROSS STITCH

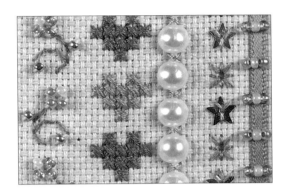

*N*ow that you have perfected all the techniques of cross stitch you may wish to add texture and sparkle to your work by incorporating ribbons, beads, lace and sequins into the stitching. Ribbons can not only be couched with cross stitches to the surface of the fabric where they form lines of solid colour but can also be further ornamented with seed beads. Larger beads can add texture and colour, whilst sequins provide sparkle. To add extra froth, lace can be applied to the surface of the fabric by cross stitching into the straight edge of the lace.

## TEXTURED SAMPLER
*Finished Size: This will depend on your frame*

Choose a pretty frame and fill it with rows of the pattern to make a delectable sampler. When you have mastered the techniques you could stitch favourite rows onto small pieces of fabric to mount as greetings cards. Try changing the colour scheme and choice of ornamentation – the possibilities are endless.

I worked my sampler on Zweigart 22 count Oslo in Cream, but you may prefer to choose an alternative fabric. Quantities for the ornamentation will depend on the size of your frame.

Frames can be painted to match your embroidery; spray them outdoors with car spray paints.

### You Will Need
- *A frame for the finished work*
- *Evenweave fabric, sufficient to fill the frame plus 2in (5cm) all round for turnings*
- *Embroidery hoop (large enough to contain the whole design)*
- *Stranded cottons as in the colour key*
- *Tapestry needles, sizes 24 and 26*
- *Beading needle, size 10*
- *White sewing cotton*
- *Mill Hill Glass Seed Bead mini-pack containing Blue (00168), Cream (02001), Green (00561) and Pink (02005)*
- *Offray 3mm ribbon, colour Rosy-Mauve (165)*
- *White cotton lace, ½in (1.25cm) wide (choose a lace with regular holes along the straight edge)*
- *³⁄₁₆in (5mm) opalescent heart-shaped beads*
- *³⁄₁₆in (5mm) white ric-rac braid*
- *³⁄₁₆in (5mm) silver star-shaped sequins*
- *Pearl beading*

**1** Prepare the fabric for work and mount it in the hoop. *Row 1* Using a knotless start (pg24) and starting with the large hearts, work straightforward cross stitch.

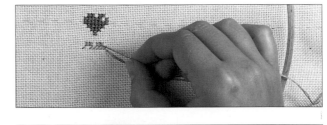

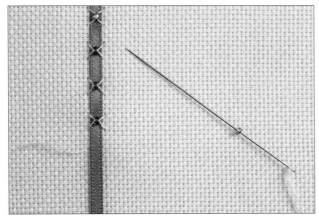

**2** *Row 2* Cut a length of 3mm ribbon and place it on the surface of the fabric. Using a beading needle and one strand of cream stranded cotton bring the needle out at the correct position, as shown on the chart, to one side of the ribbon. Thread a blue seed bead onto the stranded cotton and insert the needle into the correct position on the other side of

the ribbon to form the first half of a large cross stitch. Bring the needle out again, ready to complete the cross stitch. Put the needle through the seed bead again in the opposite direction and pass over the ribbon to complete the stitch. The ribbon is now couched to the surface of the fabric and the couching cross stitch is embellished with a seed bead.

**3** *Row 3* Work straightforward cross stitch and back stitch for the trailing flowers.

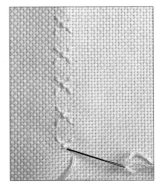

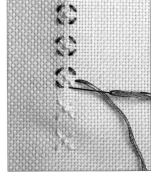

## *Perfectionist's Corner*

*When stitching with a beading needle you will find that the fine, sharp point of the needle is prone to split the threads of the fabric. In order to ensure that the thread is delivered to the hole correctly, try working with the beading needle upside-down. This entails working with the threaded eye of the needle and care is needed to avoid pricking oneself with the sharp end.*

**4** *Row 4* On each repeat, work the centre cross stitch followed by the four straight corner stitches using three strands of cream stranded cotton. Then, using three strands of blue stranded cotton, cross each of the corner stitches to form bi-coloured cross stitches.

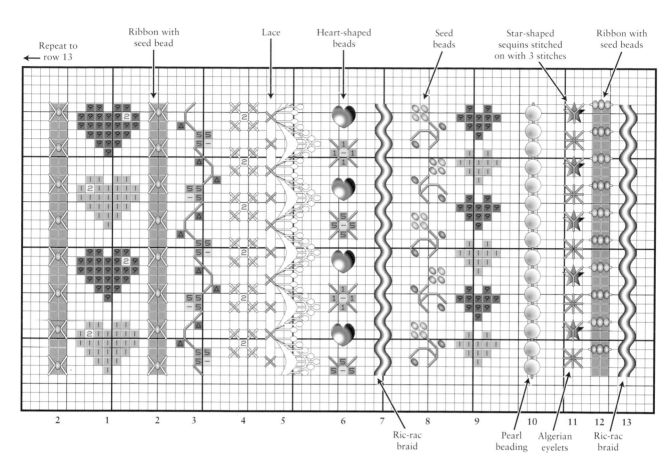

Repeat to
← row 13

Ribbon with
seed bead

Lace

Heart-shaped
beads

Seed
beads

Star-shaped
sequins stitched
on with 3 stitches

Ribbon with
seed beads

2    1    2    3    4    5    6    7    8    9    10    11    12    13

Ric-rac
braid

Pearl
beading

Algerian
eyelets

Ric-rac
braid

## TEXTURED SAMPLER

### *Colour Key*

DMC/Anchor
Cross stitch

| | |
|---|---|
| – – | 677/886 |
| I I | 932/1033 |
| 1 1 | 3727/1016 |
| 2 2 | 712/926 |
| 5 5 | 3042/870 |
| 9 9 | 931/1034 |
| △ △ | 502/876 |
| ▓ | Ribbon |

| | |
|---|---|
| ══ | 502/876 |
| ══ | 712/926 |
| ══ | 316/1017 |
| ══ | 932/1033 |

### NOTES

Work all cross stitches with three strands of stranded cotton. Use two strands for back stitch and one strand for beads and sequins.

Work enough of each row of the pattern to fill your frame. Check that your rows are long enough by holding the frame face down on the work as each row nears completion. Be generous with the number of repeats you work, even if some of your work is swallowed up in the framing, it is better to have too much rather than not enough to fill the frame.

When one side of the pattern is complete work the mirror image to fill the other half of the design.

**5** *Row 5* Using three strands of pink cotton, stitch the white cotton lace to the fabric using cross stitches at regular intervals along the straight edge of the lace.

**6** *Row 6* Stitch the flowers in cross stitch and back stitch. Attach the pearlised heart beads between the flowers using one strand of cream stranded cotton.

**7** *Row 7* Stitch a length of white ric-rac braid into position using white sewing cotton and tiny, invisible back stitches.

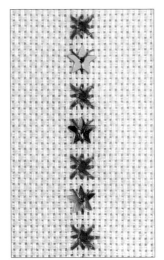
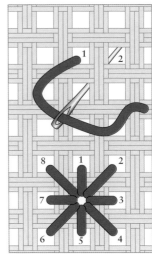

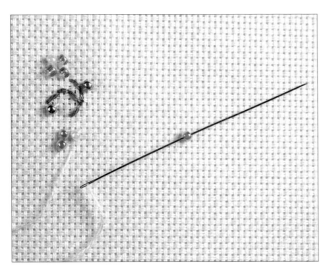

**8** *Row 8* Using a beading needle and one strand of cream stranded cotton, stitch the seed beads into the positions shown on the chart. Use half cross stitches to attach them and, to ensure that all the beads lie in the same direction, be consistent in the direction of stitching the half cross stitches.

**9** *Row 9* Stitch the small hearts following the chart, using straightforward cross stitch.

**10** *Row 10* Using three strands of pink stranded cotton, couch a length of pearl beading with cross stitches to the fabric at regular intervals between pearls.

**11** *Row 11* Attach the star-shaped sequins using one strand of blue stranded cotton and the size 26 tapestry needle. Work three straight stitches into the central hole of each sequin following the directions shown on the chart. Work Algerian eyelets between the sequins, using two strands of pink stranded cotton. Work each stitch in turn, starting at 1, into the central hole (see diagram above). Tug slightly on the thread after each stitch to slightly enlarge the hole and produce a lacy effect.

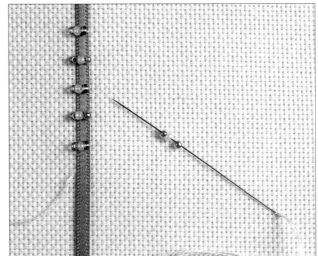

**12** *Row 12* Work as Step 2 (Row 2), but for variety couch down the ribbon with straight stitches which hold three seed beads.

**13** *Row 13* Repeat Step 7 (Row 7), stitching a length of white ric-rac braid into position using white sewing thread and tiny back stitches.

**14** When all the stitching is complete remove the work from the hoop and frame it in your chosen frame.

## TARTAN CHRISTMAS FRAME

*Revamp the textured design by stitching on 22 count Zweigart Hardanger, in Christmas Red. Follow the instructions for working the heart-shaped frame but substitute a circular green fame and Christmassy-coloured threads (see chart, pg115). Tiny jingle bells replace the heart-shaped beads while tartan ribbon, gathered into a ruffle, is glued to the back of the frame.*

perforated paper (see Skill 7 to recap working with perforated paper). Using the cover of the ruler as a guide, cut out a piece of plain, white backing paper to fit. Similarly, cut the perforated paper to fit the aperture. Place the backing paper in the ruler, then the embroidery, face up. Snap one end of the cover into place, bend the cover (it is flexible) and slot the other end into place. The flatter your work is on the reverse, the better the fit.

## FRAMING YOUR WORK
Designs which are designated as greetings cards, pot-pourri sachets and other unprotected stitching, can all be framed for wall display. A sympathetic choice of frame can enhance a design and give it a totally new look, as can be seen in the Lavender Bag design on pg54. It is best to choose a framer who specialises in framing embroidery. Ensure that the work will be mounted onto acid-free card to prevent 'foxing' (small brown spots which appear in time, mark the fabric and ruin its appearance).

Use a mount wherever possible to prevent the glass from flattening the surface of the embroidery, or ask the framer to raise the glass by placing thin strips of card around the edge of the frame where the overlap will hide them. Use plain or non-reflective glass, whichever you prefer, but plain glass gives a better view of your masterpiece. Avoid hanging framed work in full sun because the bright light will fade the threads and rot the fabric.

### Flexi-hoop Picture
A flexi-hoop can be used as a decorative frame as seen on pg108. Here the Treasure Box design has been adapted and worked on navy 14 count Aida to fit a 3in (7.5cm) red flexi-hoop. The fabric was cut to a 5 x 5in (13 x 13cm) piece and laid over the inner hoop. The outer hoop was eased over the fabric and the inner hoop until it snapped into place, making sure that the threads of the fabric were straight in relation to the hanger at the top of the hoop. When the work was complete, the excess

fabric was trimmed to ½in (1.25cm). A fine running stitch was worked around the edge of the fabric, and the thread pulled up to draw the gathers towards the centre of the back of the flexi-hoop. The threads were finished off tautly. The back of the work was covered by gluing on a circle of felt.

## USING COMMERCIAL MOUNTS
A glance through a mount supplier's catalogue will spark off many new ideas for presenting your work – key tags, napkin holders, bowls, cards, coasters, paperweights – the list is excitingly long. But before rushing to place an order, do check that your chosen design will fit the mount (see pg12). There are several examples throughout the book of these commercially made products, such as the napkin holder on pg68, derived from the Christmas Heart-Shaped Baskets design. Further ideas follow on how to display your work in some of the mounts available commercially.

### Bowl Lids
Bowls in all shapes and sizes, in porcelain, glass, wood or metal are available nowadays. The lids are supplied as blanks and can be filled with pressed flowers, lace or embroidery. Examples in this book are the tiny porcelain bowl design, adapted from the Christmas Heart-Shaped Baskets (pg71); the heart-shaped porcelain bowl (pg74) and the oval porcelain bowl using the Zodiac designs from pg99.

Manufacturers normally provide instructions for mounting embroidery into bowl lids but instructions are also provided here. Generally, you will first need to back your stitched piece with iron-on Vilene, to prevent fraying when you cut the work to fit the lid. Along with the bowl and lid, most manufacturers supply an acetate disc, a sponge disc, a paper disc, a metal locking disc and a lid liner. Lay the acetate disc over the right side of your work and centralise it by counting how many empty blocks show under the acetate. Make sure that you have the same number of unworked blocks at the top as you have at the bottom, and an equal number on each side.

Mark around the edge of the acetate with a pencil to give a cutting line (see pg99, Step 8).

Cut out the embroidery along the cutting line, then place the acetate disc into the lid, followed by the embroidery, then the sponge disc. Check that the embroidery is correctly displayed and then push home the metal locking plate. Finally, add the lid liner, holding it in place with a little glue if necessary.

## Coaster
To display your work in a coaster, first back the embroidery with iron-on Vilene to prevent fraying. Place the backing plate of the coaster centrally over the work and draw around it with a pencil. Cut the work out along the pencil line and place it in the coaster. Push home the backing plate to finish.

## Paperweight
Attractive paperweights can be bought in which to display cross stitch designs. When the embroidery is complete, back with iron-on Vilene. Lay the paper

*An everyday heart design has been used in different ways and with different colours for these items (see chart pg113). A 2½ x 2¼in (6.5 x 5.5cm) heart-shaped paperweight frames a pastel version of the design. Work with care on cream 22 count Zweigart Oslo, as the thick glass of the paperweight magnifies the stitching slightly, so every twist on the thread will show. The same heart design has been worked in primary colours over waste canvas to add a special touch to a pair of children's dungarees. For everyday clothes it is important to test selected threads for colour fastness (see boxed text pg109).*

disc (supplied with the paperweight) on a dark surface, or against a window during daylight. Centre the embroidery right side up on top of the disc, which will show through the work. Pencil the outline of the disc onto the fabric. Cut out and place the design in the paperweight. Place the paper disc over the back of the embroidery and cover with the sticky backing disc (which can be repositioned if necessary).

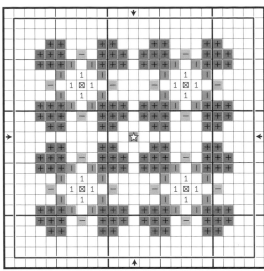

## NAPKIN HOLDERS

(photos pgs68 & 71)

*Colour Key*

DMC/Anchor
Cross stitch

| | |
|---|---|
| ㄱㄱ | 995/410 |
| – – | 554/96 |
| I I | 992/187 |
| 1 1 | Blanc/1 |
| = = | 321/9046 |
| + + | 603/62 |
| ⁄⁄ | 699/923 |
| ⊠ ⊠ | 744/301 |
| ✳ ✳ | 726/295 |

—— Cutting lines

☆ Middle point

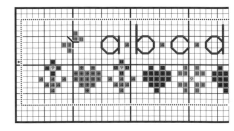

## RULER (photo pg41)

*Colour Key*

DMC/Anchor
Cross stitch

| | | | |
|---|---|---|---|
| 2 2 | Blanc/1 | II II | 798/131 |
| 3 3 | 310/403 | = = | 321/9046 |
| 4 4 | 699/923 | + + | 3607/87 |
| 5 5 | 400/351 | H H | 333/119 |
| 9 9 | 726/295 | | |

Backstitch

—— 310/403 ⋯⋯⋯ Cutting line
—— 321/9046 ☆ Middle point

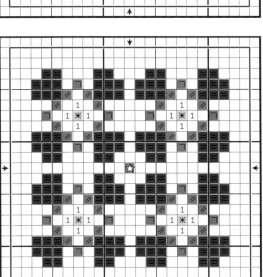

## PORCELAIN BOWL (photo pg71)

*Colour Key*

DMC/Anchor
Cross stitch

| | |
|---|---|
| ㄱㄱ | 340/118 |
| 1 1 | Blanc/1 |
| = = | 3609/85 |
| ⁄⁄ | 959/186 |
| ✳ ✳ | 744/301 |
| ☆ | Middle point |

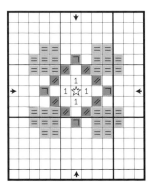

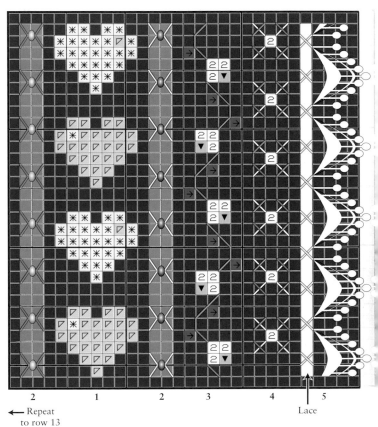

← Repeat
to row 13

2   1   2   3   4   5

Lace

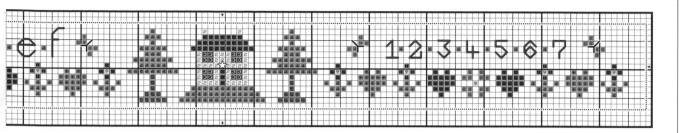

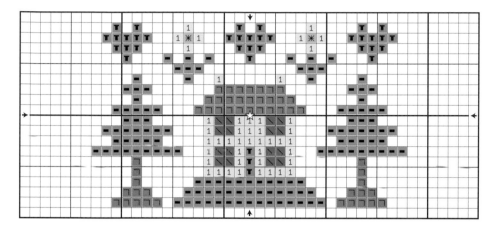

## KEY TAG (photo pg41)
### *Colour Key*

|  | DMC/Anchor |
|---|---|
|  | Cross stitch |
| ⅂⅂ | 781/309 |
| 1 1 | Ecru/926 |
| ◣◣ | 3768/779 |
| ▬ ▬ | 502/876 |
| ✳ ✳ | 833/907 |
| T T | 356/1013 |
|  |  |
| ☆ | Middle point |

## TARTAN CHRISTMAS FRAME
(photo pg107)
### *Colour Key*

|  | DMC/Anchor |
|---|---|
|  | Cross stitch |
| 2 2 | Blanc/1 |
| ▽ ▽ | DMC light silver thread |
| ✕ ✕ | 995/410 |
|  | Red fabric |
| → → | 699/923 |
|  | Christmas green ribbon |
| ✳ ✳ | DMC light gold thread |
| ▼ ▼ | 676/891 |
|  |  |
| — | DMC light gold thread |
| — | 699/923 |
| — | Blanc/1 |
| — | 995/410 |

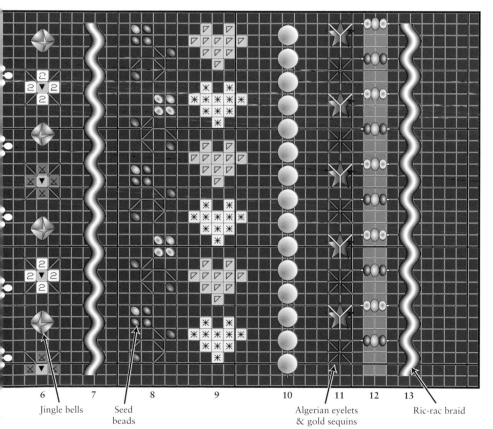

6  7  8  9  10  11  12  13

Jingle bells  Seed beads  Algerian eyelets & gold sequins  Ric-rac braid

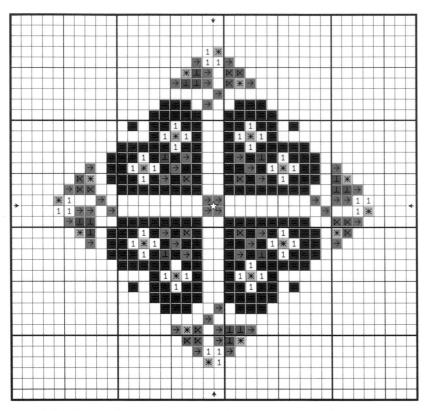

## COASTER, SPECTACLES CASE & FLEXI-HOOP PICTURE (photo pg108)
### *Colour Key*

DMC/Anchor
Cross stitch

| | |
|---|---|
| 1 1 | Blanc/1 |
| ▬▬ | 321/9046 |
| ⋉⋉ | 995/410 |
| ⊥⊥ | 3607/87 |
| →→ | 699/923 |
| ✳✳ | 726/295 |

☆　　　Middle point

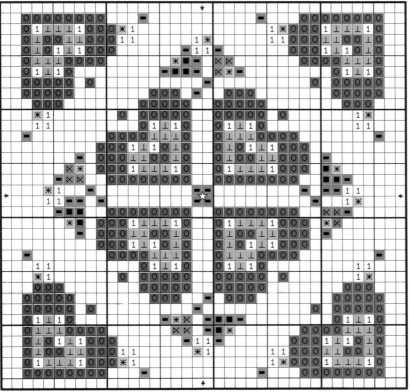

## VALENTINE CARD
(photo pg66)
### *Colour Key*

DMC/Anchor
Cross stitch

| | |
|---|---|
| 1 1 | Blanc/1 |
| ⋉⋉ | 809/130 |
| O O | 603/62 |
| ⊥⊥ | 605/50 |
| ▬▬ | 992/187 |
| ✳✳ | 744/301 |
| ■■ | 554/96 |

☆　　　Middle point

# THE GOLDEN RULES
# OF CROSS STITCH

- Wash hands before stitching and keep work clean between embroidery sessions.

- Oversew the edges of fabric to prevent fraying.

- Work in an embroidery hoop or frame whenever possible.

- Keep all top stitches lying in the same direction.

- Do not allow twists to develop on the thread.

- Do not jump thread across the back of bare fabric.

- Trim all ends neatly, close to the fabric.

- Only cut embroidery thread with embroidery scissors.

- Do not use knots to start or finish a thread.

- Work in good light and check work frequently for mistakes.

- Never fold your work, always roll it to avoid stubborn creases.

- Press finished embroidery face down on a thick, white terry towel to avoid crushing the stitches.

| Fabric | Needle size | No of strands | Fabric | Needle size | No of strands |
|---|---|---|---|---|---|
| 6 count Binca | 20 | 6 | 25 count Dublin | 24 | 3 |
| 8 count Aida | 22 | 4 | 27 count Linda | 26 | 2 |
| 11 count Aida | 24 | 3 | 28 count Quaker cloth | 26 | 2 |
| 14 count Aida | 26 | 2 | 28 count Jobelan | 26 | 2 |
| 16 count Aida | 26 | 2 | 32 count Belfast | 26 | 2 |
| 18 count Aida | 26/28 | 2 | 36 count Edinburgh | 26/28 | 2 |
| 20 count Bellana | 24 | 3 | 55 count Kingston | 28 | 1 |
| 22 count Oslo | 24 | 3 | | | |

*NOTE Add an extra strand of stranded cotton to the needle if the tension of your stitching does not give sufficient coverage of the fabric.*

# INDEX